Faulkner's Mississippi

Faulkner's Mississippi

Text by Willie Morris

Photographs by William Eggleston

Oxmoor
House.

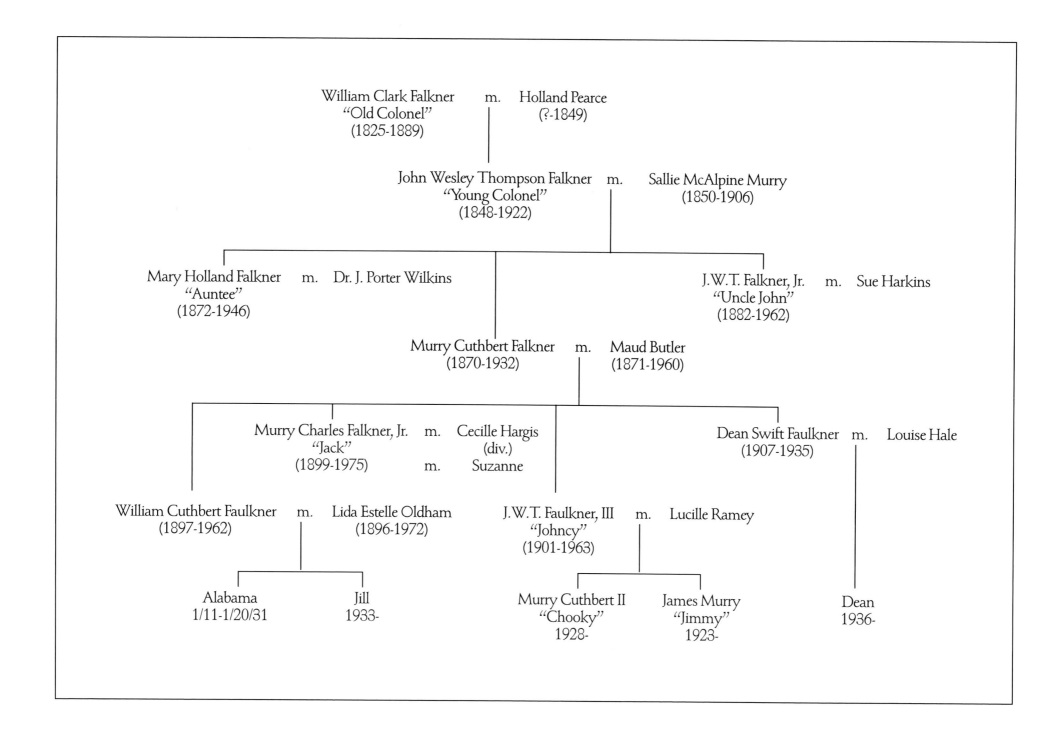

William Clark Falkner   m.   Holland Pearce
"Old Colonel"   (?-1849)
(1825-1889)

John Wesley Thompson Falkner   m.   Sallie McAlpine Murry
"Young Colonel"   (1850-1906)
(1848-1922)

Mary Holland Falkner   m.   Dr. J. Porter Wilkins   J.W.T. Falkner, Jr.   m.   Sue Harkins
"Auntee"   "Uncle John"
(1872-1946)   (1882-1962)

Murry Cuthbert Falkner   m.   Maud Butler
(1870-1932)   (1871-1960)

Murry Charles Falkner, Jr.   m.   Cecille Hargis   Dean Swift Faulkner   m.   Louise Hale
"Jack"   (div.)   (1907-1935)
(1899-1975)   m.   Suzanne

William Cuthbert Faulkner   m.   Lida Estelle Oldham   J.W.T. Faulkner, III   m.   Lucille Ramey
(1897-1962)   (1896-1972)   "Johncy"
         (1901-1963)

Alabama   Jill   Murry Cuthbert II   James Murry   Dean
1/11-1/20/31   1933-   "Chooky"   "Jimmy"   1936-
         1928-   1923-

Portrait of the Artist

HIS SPIRIT IS STILL HERE, OF COURSE: IN the woodsmoke of November from the forlorn country shacks, in the fireflies in driftless random in the town in June, in the summer wisteria on the greenswards and the odor of verbena, in the ruined old mansions in the Yocona bottoms, in the echoes of an axe on wood and of dogs barking far away, in the languid human commerce on the courthouse square, in the aged whites and blacks bantering on the brick wall beside the jail.

William Faulkner's imaginative, intuitive cosmos—Yoknapatawpha County—was one of the most convincing ever conceived by a writer. His own "little postage stamp of native soil," as he called it, was a spiritual kingdom that he transmuted into a microcosm not only of the South but also of the human race. More than any other American novelist, with the possible exception of Hawthorne, he stayed close to home. In his youth there were a few months in the East, in New Orleans, in Europe, but in the 1920s something turned in him; he began to realize the advantages of using the place where he had been reared as the setting for much of his fiction. Despite his later sojourns in Hollywood and in Charlottesville, Virginia, his physical and emotional fidelity to Oxford and to Mississippi, to the land and the people that shaped him, was at the core of his being, so that today Oxford and the real county—Lafayette—are the most tangibly, palpably connected to one writer's soul of any locale in America.

In the beginning it was virgin—to the west, along the Big Black River, the alluvial swamps threaded by black, almost motionless bayous and impenetrable with cane and buckvine and cypress and ash and oak and gum. . . . This land, this South, for which God has done so much, with woods for game and streams for fish and deep rich soil for seed and lush springs to sprout it and long summers to mature it and serene falls to harvest it and short mild winters for men and animals. . . . That's the trouble with this country. Everything, weather, all, hangs on too long. Like our rivers, our land: opaque, slow, violent; shaping and creating the life of man in its implacable and brooding image. . . .

Words like these first drew me to Faulkner when I was a homesick Mississippi boy at the University of Texas in the 1950s. At first I was awestruck, mesmerized, then saturated. His world of Sartorises and Snopeses, Compsons and Varners, Beauchamps and McCaslins, dogs and mules and woodlands and swamp bottoms was my world, too. My own Yazoo City was only 120 miles from his fictional Jefferson. Then, after a while, I became frightened, a fear that seeped deep into my blood and left me nearly breathless with doubt. I thought I wanted to be a writer. How could one ever be as good as this man? What did Flannery O'Connor mean when she said to get off the tracks quickly when the Dixie Limited came roaring through?

Finally I made my private truce with Mr. Bill, as many of us have. I never met him. There were too many years between us. But I know him. After a long time in the East, I now live in his town. Twenty-five years ago this might have intimidated me, but today I draw a rare sustenance and serenity in dwelling among his people and places. I have learned from them.

It was Sherwood Anderson, in New Orleans in 1925, who encouraged the young writer to return home and write of what he knew. He would learn, through much labor, "that by sublimating the actual into the apocryphal I would have complete liberty to use whatever talent I might have to its absolute top . . . so I created a cosmos of my own." The boundaries of Yoknapatawpha County—15,611 people over 2,400 square miles, "William Faulkner, sole owner and proprietor" as he whimsically signed a map he once drew of these environs—overlaps the real terrain of Mississippi like a mythical cloudbank, exerting upon it a nearly relentless tyranny—"All the separate works," as Malcolm Cowley wrote, "are like blocks of marble from the same quarry: they show the veins and faults of the mother rock." Faulkner's brother John, who survived him by a year, sat on the steps of the funeral home waiting for William's body to be brought there.

I could see the section of the Square across which Joe Christmas was led from the jail to the courthouse where, manacled, he had broken away from his guard and run, chased by Percy Grimm on his commandeered bicycle. And on below the sheriff's house, facing the very road that ran under my feet, was the small frame building where Preacher Hightower lived and from the front window of which he watched at dusk each evening as the ghost cavalry swept past to the sound of falling trumpets. Everywhere I looked there was Bill and his stories.

William Faulkner was a small man, about five feet six, but his facial expression and the set of his head and neck and shoulders, especially in his later years, gave the impression of greater size. His voice was soft and whispery but had carrying power, and he spoke fast. His laugh was a chuckle, almost a snort. "I don't think he knew how to laugh," his nephew Jimmy Faulkner would recall. "When he got tickled all he could do was

chuckle. I could tell when he was supposed to be laughing by watching his eyes. They would crinkle at the corners and sparkle. His eyes told more about his moods than anything else about him. When he was mad they would turn to a flashing black, but during his happy times they were a soft brown."

"He seemed to belong outdoors," his niece Dean remembers. "His skin was weathered, tan, slightly wrinkled, and he smelled of horses and leather, cedars and sunshine, pipe tobacco and bourbon. The fine lines around his eyes were traced by smiles and sadness."

He was born September 25, 1897, died July 6, 1962. (Fitzgerald was born in 1896, Hemingway in 1899, Wolfe in 1900, Steinbeck in 1902.) His father owned a livery stable, then a hardware store, and later was the secretary and business manager of the University of Mississippi—Ole Miss. He was exceptionally close to his mother, but between him and the father there was a cool distance. The elder Falkner was an uncompromising man of limited affection. William's playmates were his brothers and cousins and neighborhood children and the black children of the servants. The old black retainer, Mammy Caroline Barr, was a second mother. His relationship to her was very close, a love that deepened when he was grown and that in later life was almost worshipful. "Mammy was not considered a servant by the family or by herself," brother Murry wrote.

Her small, old-fashioned rocking chair was for her alone and always beside the fireplace. There she would sit in the evenings, as much a member of the family as the rest of us, high-button shoes (how small they were) polished and glistening in the dancing glow of the flames in the open grate, her box of snuff in place on the mantel just above her head, a good layer of it tucked beneath her lower lip and her ''snuff stick'' held firmly in her mouth....

In the fall we would return to the woods and gather hickory nuts and walnuts which we would take to Mammy's cabin in our back yard. Mother would furnish us with some

big peppermint sticks; Mammy would build a big fire; and we would eat and talk the rest of the day. Here, as I recall it, Bill began telling some tales of his own, and they were good ones, too. Some of them even stopped Mammy...a past master in the field if ever there was one.

When she died in 1940 at age one hundred William delivered her eulogy. "To Mammy I came to represent the head of that family to which she had given a half century of fidelity and devotion...She assumed cares and griefs which were not even her cares and griefs...From her I learned to tell the truth, to refrain from waste, to be considerate of the weak and respectful to age." Later, in *Go Down, Moses,* he wrote this dedication:

To Mammy
Caroline Barr
Mississippi
(1840-1940)

*Who was born in slavery and who gave to my family
a fidelity without stint or calculation of recompense and to my childhood
an immeasurable devotion and love.*

Although he read a great deal in his youth, he was not considered a bookworm, and he was impatient with school. Oxford did not have a public library then, but his mother loved books and literature. There was an impressive library in their home, and from the earliest years she encouraged her boys to read: James Fenimore Cooper, Dickens, Grimm's fairy tales, Mark Twain, and later, Conrad, Poe, Balzac, Fielding, Hugo, Shakespeare, Kipling, Voltaire. As with Mammy Callie, he would sit at his grandfather John Wesley Thompson Falkner's knee and listen to his tales of the Civil War, such as of

Nathan Bedford Forrest's raiding the Gayoso Hotel in Memphis, spurring his horse into the lobby and forcing a Yankee general to escape out a window in his underwear. This oral, story-telling tradition of Scotch-Irish ancestry helped shape his imagination and made him long for adventure. He in turn would pass along these stories, and others of his own imaginings, to his daughter Jill, his step-granddaughter Vicki, and his niece Dean.

About 1,000 people lived in Oxford in those maiden years of the twentieth century. "How kind they were," Murry remembered, "those years of long ago; how gentle the life and how pleasant the memories of it." It was a self-sufficient life, touched with a profound feel of community and belonging, the woods enclosing the town, the lush pastures, the deep quiet of the boyhood nights. Years later people would remember seeing William as a small child walking with Mammy Callie through the streets of the indolent, drowsing town. She would say: "Get up here on this sidewalk, Billy," and he would shout, "I ain't gonna do it," and walk in the dust of the road.

William was the eldest of the four brothers: then John and Murry, and Dean, who did not come along until 1907. William was the leader, and all of them rode ponies and built treehouses and were infatuated with trains and the early airplanes and automobiles. Their grandfather, a banker known as the Young Colonel, owned a 1909 Buick touring car. He employed a black driver named Chess, and the boys would accompany them on day-long drives to the Peabody in Memphis seventy or so miles away over the rutted dirt roads made even more hazardous by the ubiquitous Mississippi mud, and the opportunistic farmers along the route would charge three dollars to tow out the stricken Buick with their mules in harness. In those golden years of railroads the Illinois Central had a branch line through the town with several daily passenger trains and freights, and the boys spent countless hours at the depot. Murry wrote:

Every engineer had his own assigned locomotive and his own distinctive touch to the beautiful whistle on it; and we knew them all, by sight and sound. Often we could hear one laboring up Thacker's Mountain seven miles south of town. Then, as it began the gentle descent to the level track leading into town, its exhaust would quicken to a rapid beat and we knew that the soul-lilting wail of the whistle would quickly follow. As soon as we heard it we could declare without possibility of error, for instance, "That's Mr. Markette with number 849," or "That's Mr. McLeod with number 912," and we were never mistaken. . . .

The brothers were good athletes. William played quarterback for Oxford High School, where he broke his nose. Often they whiled away the dallying summer days on the University golf course, a most unaccountable stretch of terrain which was in considerable measure a cow pasture, the only places without grass being the greens, which were nothing but sand, and they carried their own shovels and rakes to remove the cow droppings and to make their own putting contours.

Bill Faulkner loved baseball, and as youths the brothers played various odd adaptations of the grand pastime. When they were little they devised a moveable version. The game shifted constantly from one side of town to the other, utilizing one vacant lot after another in this bizarre marathon ritual. They likewise organized games in their big side yard, usually of their own age group, but as Murry recalled "not infrequently older boys and even some grown men would join in the fun getting away from their labors in town to relax in the late hours of the long summer afternoons. They would arrive singly or in groups and watch us scampering about our improvised diamond as they shed their ties and rolled up their sleeves. Then Mr. Neilson would call out, 'Me and Ed and Jim will take on the Falkner boys!'"

When they were older the brothers played for the Methodists, in what was known as "The Church League," against the Baptists, Presbyterians,

and Episcopalians, and all ages were eligible to play if they went to church—Bill was the pitcher, John the shortstop, Murry the catcher, young Dean the center fielder. The league was eventually disbanded, however, when the churches started bringing in out-of-town ringers. "The whole business lasted only a year or two," one of the participants remembered, "because it got too competitive. Grown men fought like cats and dogs, even the preachers . . . ." A number of years later, when William was living in New Haven, Connecticut, working as a clerk for the Winchester Arms Company, he sent his youngest brother Dean drawings he had done of football and baseball players. Even as late as the 1950s people saw him at Ole Miss baseball games, sitting dapperly on the top row of the bleachers on the third base side in seersucker suit and Panama hat.

Community. Fellowship. Belonging. Lewis P. Simpson has observed of these growing up years an arresting irony. "In the Yoknapatawpha stories we are nearly always aware of strong tensions growing either out of the threats or the facts of irreversible change in a traditional social structure. Yoknapatawpha is haunted by the mood of estrangement and alienation." The Oxford of the artist's youth, on the other hand, was filled with a strong sense of identity. "Everybody and everything in this place had an individual meaning. Community was based on a series of interwoven individual relationships maintained in a society that . . . was more the product of frontier democratic improvisation and compromise than the traditional order we encounter in the Yoknapatawpha world."

It would someday be the artist, in his solitary heart, who would transform the simpler, evanescent retrospective into the darker universal.

All his life he loved to ride horses, which were always throwing him, and as a grown man he owned a sailboat and took pride in being a sailor. He adored, of course, to hunt in the big, vanishing woods, but he was not a particularly good shot. In Virginia, years later, he rode to the hounds. He loved dogs and understood them as much as he did mules. "Some Homer of the cottonfields should sing the saga of the mule and his place in the South. He it was, more than any one creature or thing, who . . . won the prone South from beneath the iron heel of Reconstruction . . . by sheer and vindictive patience." From the pastoral years of pre-World War I Oxford he developed an admiration and compassion for animals, and an observant eye for their strengths and foibles. "A horse ain't got much sense," he judged. "A mule's got more sense. A mule can take care of himself and you, too. Actually, a rat has the most sense of nonhuman animals, then a dog, then a cat, then a mule and then a horse."

As for the girls of his youth, he admired them but was habitually shy, then and later. Long before he became a writer, he was in love with his future wife, Estelle, a fragile, popular beauty one and a half years his senior. But her parents considered him undeserving and without promise, and she married someone else, bore two children, then eventually was divorced and married him. He would not be a particularly good husband and had a number of affairs—in New York, Memphis, Hollywood—often with much younger women, later chronicled by either the women or third parties, or both, and which this writer chooses not to detail.

He enjoyed the company of children. He relished conversational games: who were the twelve Caesars? If you were a vegetable, which would you prefer to be, and why?

He could be curt and rude and cutting, even among his family. He had no patience with cruel buffoons in any locale. To him, I sense, manners had nothing to do with social class but with the way people behaved—their quintessential character. When he went to the University of Virginia in his

*T*he right disjointed marble columns were landed from an Italian ship at New Orleans, into a steamboat up the Mississippi...the two identical four-column porticoes, one on the north and one on the south, each with its balcony of wrought-iron New Orleans grillwork, on one of which—the south one—in 1861 Sartoris would stand in the first Confederate uniform....

From Requiem For A Nun

declining years, he said, with considerable irony, that he admired Virginians because they were snobs, bound by manners, tradition, reserve, and, of course, superiority. "Most deep Southerners revere Virginia," Shelby Foote of Mississippi has correctly reckoned. "Their reverence even survives a trip there. Any folks of quality, black or white, always insist their ancestors landed there. I suppose being from Virginia means that you're not a Snopes [Faulkner's name for white trash]." I believe he always knew, deep down, that he was born to be a great writer, and I am certain he considered himself a Sartoris, an aristocrat, a fallen patrician, striving to regain the grandeur of his great-grandfather W.C. Falkner. (W.C. had dropped the *u* from the surname, and William reinserted it.)

The Old Colonel, as W.C. was known, of Ripley, in the northeast section of the state where Mississippi assumes a curious, abrupt savor of the mountains, was of vaunted proportions: duelist, soldier, railroad builder, lawyer, planter, writer. He rode with Nathan Bedford Forrest, organized and for a while commanded the Second Mississippi Infantry, and eventually became the unwavering prototype for his great-grandson's Colonel John Sartoris. He authored several books, including a best-selling novel called *The White Rose of Memphis*, which he claimed to have written to subsidize the building of his railroad from Pontotoc, Mississippi, to Middleton, Tennessee. He was murdered in the year 1889 by his business partner, R.J. Thurmond, on the Tippah County square, and today his majestic stone column with his life-sized statue atop it, gently specked with lichen, commands the old Ripley cemetery with histrionic authority as he gazes in replica toward the tracks of his own railroad and a modern Pizza Hut just beyond it. "He stood on a stone pedestal, in his frock coat and bareheaded, one leg slightly advanced," the great-grandson would write in *Sartoris*. "His head was lifted a little in that gesture of haughty pride which repeated itself generation after generation

with a fateful fidelity, his back to the world and his carven eyes gazing out across the valley where his railroad ran, and the blue changeless hills beyond, and beyond that, the ramparts of infinity itself." All of this affected William, who set out to emulate that immutable heritage of the country squire, the planter with the big house, and who was later wont to say that he wrote books to support his own modest and unlucrative farm in the unregenerate hills of Beat Two, Lafayette County.

In that aristocratic mold William Faulkner was a diffident man, his sense of privacy sacrosanct and legendary, wrapped in what a friend from his Hollywood days would call "his air of frigid inviolability." There was a No Trespassing sign on the lane leading to his house. In Oxford, you could walk by him on the square and say hello, and he would look right through you, although the next day he might stop for an amiable conversation. "Everybody has written that he was antisocial, aloof," his friend and personal doctor Chester McLarty says. "The truth is, he was really a very shy man, except with children and old people. He had an armor toward intellectuals, and especially toward university people." In private intercourse on his home grounds he was quiet, unpretentious, often gracious and charming, but he vilified the abrupt intrusions. James Silver, the Ole Miss historian, was at Faulkner's dinner table in Oxford one evening in the 1950s when the host was summoned by a telephone call from Edward R. Murrow of CBS in New York. He folded his napkin, went to the pantry telephone, and said, "This is William Faulkner. I am at dinner. Good night." Nor is it apocryphal that in Charlottesville he rejected an invitation by the Kennedy White House honoring the Nobel laureates on the grounds that it was too far to go for dinner. Once a news reporter asked him, "Mr. Faulkner, what do you think is decadent in society today?" and he said, "What you're doing, Miss."

The fellow Mississippian Tennessee Williams met him on three occasions.

He seemed as shy as imaginable. He was with a very beautiful girl, and he could only talk in whispers to her. I didn't try to draw him into a conversation. The second meeting was in Paris and a very beautiful girl was with him again. Again, there was the situation of his looking down, not up, and not talking. I had that situation, too: it's very hard for me to talk sometimes, and one of my phobias is that I will not be able to talk. But Faulkner actually didn't talk at all. And finally I felt, you know, that I had to talk directly to him. So I did. I talked to Faulkner directly. Suddenly he lifted his eyes, and I saw such suffering in them that I felt tears coming into my eyes.

He was terrified of the human breed *en masse*. At a cocktail party he turned to Joseph Blotner, who would eventually be his eminent biographer: "I gotta get outa here. My claustrophobia is closing in on me." At the Commodore Hotel in New York in 1955, a journalist covering his acceptance speech before an audience of several hundred reported, "As his name was called, summoning him to the platform, every person in that hall leaned forward, tense with expectancy. Mr. Faulkner's frame shuddered like a child fearful of being thrown into a tub of icy water. On his face was an expression of such grimness, such resignation, as I have never seen before, and never expect to see again. It was then that I came to the conclusion that any effort to present William Faulkner in a public appearance is a disservice even to his most devoted admirers."

He was a master of reverse snobbery. He deplored the radio, and the telephone was his most unmitigating *bête noire*. "He had a natural and sustained aversion to the telephone," his brother Murry said, "anywhere, anytime, and under any conceivable circumstances." He did not own a television set, but many Sundays in the 1950s he went to Professor James Silver's house on the Ole Miss campus and watched "Car 54, Where Are You?"—and sometimes stayed to watch "Bonanza," too. "It was awful

stuff," Silver said. "He sits there in front of the TV, puffs away at his pipe, and watches and listens intently. He never says a word about the program, and when it's over he thanks me and leaves." For years he drove an ancient Ford convertible with rusted floorboards. The children remembered looking through the holes in the floorboard and seeing the street beneath. Things kept falling out: books, shirts, toys, swimming suits, fishhooks. When he had money he bought fine things: clothes, pipes, hunting gear, even an airplane. He liked fine food, fine wines and spirits. He took good care of his family, and the sweep of it included his niece, nephews, step-children, cousins, and black retainers. He was intensely loyal to those he loved.

He could be a very funny man, and also his own most efficacious myth maker. The person who wrote "Spotted Horses," surely one of the funniest stories in our literature, "Old Man," and *The Reivers* was no stranger to uproarious absurdity or to sober, straight-faced farce, with the resonances of Mark Twain. When an early interviewer asked where he was born, he said, "Born? Yes. I was born male and single and at an early age in Mississippi. I am still alive but not single. I was born of a Negro slave and an alligator." He and James Silver were riding around town in the primitive days of television and he pointed to the large number of TV aerials on roofs. "I'm willing to bet that most of those aren't attached to television sets. These folks don't own any, but they like to have their neighbors think they do. It seems that two creatures from outer space were flying over an American city, and one of 'em looked down at the roofs with the aerials and said, 'Look at all those good-looking females down there.' "

When he spoke he often lapsed into the pristine Mississippi vernacular, as educated Mississippians still do: "He ain't a-gonna stop"—"I don't aim to see it no mo' "—"I ain't a-gonna do nuthin' about it." Ben Wasson noticed when Faulkner visited New York for two months in 1931 that he talked in

three different roles, moving from one to the other depending upon the mood and circumstance: the old Southern colonel, the worldly literary figure, the colloquial dirt farmer. Of an Ole Miss friend he dropped in on years later in Greenville, a man once noted for his dry wit who had converted to religion and was a Sunday School teacher, Faulkner allowed, "I liked his dry wit better when he was a drinker than his wet wit now that he's dry."

He had thirty acres or so of woods behind his house, and people would go into them and shoot at the squirrels. He took out a paid advertisement in the local paper.

NOTICE

The posted woods on my property inside the city limits of Oxford contain several tame squirrels. Any hunter who feels himself too lacking in woodcraft and marksmanship to approach a dangerous wild squirrel might feel safe with these. These woods are a part of the pasture used by my horses and milk cow; also, the late arrival will find them already full of other hunters. He is kindly requested not to shoot either of these.

William Faulkner

At the University of Virginia in the late 1950s he appeared before a gathering of students:

Faulkner: Respectability destroys one....That is, nobody seems to be brave enough anymore to be an out-and-out blackguard or rascal, that sooner or later he's got to be respectable, and that finishes it.

Student: You said that you regard respectability as one of the prime enemies of individualism. Do you regard love as an enemy of individualism?

Faulkner: What's love got to do with respectability?

He went on horrific binges. He could be a cruel drunk, or a totally silent one, and later contrite. Those who knew him say he would almost consciously decide he was going to get drunk. And he would. His bouts of heavy drinking followed not only failures but also successes, such as the one shortly after he was told that he had won the Nobel Prize for Literature. It is likely that he drank less than was popularly rumored, but he was often treated in Memphis or at a sanitarium in Byhalia, forty-five miles north of Oxford, and that is where he died. "His own character prevented him from being what one might call a happy man," his brother Murry surmised. "His measure of life was not how long one could enjoy it, but what he did with it. Had he been given a choice between a long life without liquor or a short one with it, he would have immediately and without hesitation taken the latter, unfettered by apprehension and unconsumed with remorse." Ben Wasson recalled of their Ole Miss days, "Bill Faulkner was considered an experienced drinker who held his liquor well and also knew where and when to obtain corn liquor from friends among the 'shiners." Wasson remembered he claimed that drinking whisky alleviated the pain from the leg injury he had incurred as a pilot in World War I. His youngest brother Dean, who was a barnstorming pilot living in Memphis in the early 1930s, often took care of him when he was drinking heavily. Their mother would telephone Dean in Memphis: "William is drinking. He needs you." Dean would fly down to Oxford and remain with William as long as he needed him. Sometimes they drove alone around the countryside, but usually they would stay cloistered in William's bedroom. "When Bill was drinking," Dean's widow Louise Meadow remembers, "they stayed completely alone, and Dean never told us what went on between them." Jimmy Faulkner, the nephew, recounted a less forbidding story about William and Dean.

One spring day William appeared at Dean's apartment in Memphis with a gallon of corn whiskey under his arm. After an hour or so of matching drinks, William and Dean decided

to go down town. They put the jug in the car with them, drove down Union, and parked behind the Peabody. They were both barefooted with their pants rolled up to their knees. With William carrying the jug, they walked around the corner to the entrance to the hotel. William had decided that since he was in Memphis, he ought to do some shopping. They walked out to the policeman who was directing traffic at the corner of Second and Union and quietly placed the jug behind him on the pavement. Then, relieved that their liquor supply would be taken care of, they proceeded on their shopping expedition. . . . The jug was waiting for them when they returned two hours later.

"There's a whole lot of nourishment in an acre of corn," he would say. At his house in Oxford he served Four Roses or Old Forester to visitors and kept Jack Daniel for himself. "Civilization," he told J.R. Cofield, the Oxford photographer, "started with distillation. There's no such thing as bad whiskey. Some whiskeys just happen to be better than others. But a man shouldn't fool with booze until he's fifty; then he's a damned fool if he doesn't." In the 1930s in Mississippi, he was listed as one of the executive directors of an organization called The Crusaders, a pro-repeal group to which he had pledged his membership, he said, "one hot summer night over a bottle of gin." His support did not help; to his persistent displeasure Mississippi remained legally dry for years.

"He simply drank," his daughter Jill recalls. "If you left him alone, he would drink for days, sometimes as long as a week or ten days. And when he was ready to sober up, he would. No one else could sober him up. There was no such thing as stopping Pappy from drinking. . . . He used drinking as a safety valve. It had to come out in some way and almost invariably at the end of a book. The first few days, he'd be extremely active. He'd want to do things. And then, one morning he would be a little quieter than he had been and all of a sudden he would start on his poem that heralded one of these

bouts coming on: 'When daisies pied and violets blue and ladies' smocks all silver white, and cowslip bells with yellow hue that paint the meadow with light.' And on and on and on. And you knew that the next day he'd be drinking. That was just the beginning of it."

On the 90th anniversary of the battle of Shiloh, in 1952, the authority on that bloody event, Shelby Foote, drove him there. Faulkner was wearing a tweed suit and a hat with a feather in the side. En route they stopped in Corinth, Mississippi, on the courthouse square. Foote said to his companion, "We're going to have to get a drink somewhere, but it's Sunday; God knows where we're going to get any whiskey on Sunday morning." Right inside the front door to the old Corinth Hotel was a shoeshine stand, and a young man getting his shoes shined. Faulkner told Foote the man could find some whiskey for them—anyone getting his shoes shined on Sunday morning would know where to get it.

"I don't think so," Foote said. "I think he's probably on the way to church."

"Why don't you step in there and ask him?" Faulkner suggested.

Foote did so. "Excuse me," he asked. "My friend and I are strangers here, and we were wondering where we could get a drink. Could you tell me where the bootlegger is?"

And the man said, "Well, I was fixing to go out there myself. If you could give me a ride, I'll show you the way."

After Estelle Oldham's parents refused to allow her to marry him, she married a businessman named Cornell Franklin and moved to China.

Finally he told himself that he hated her, that he would go away; finally he was going to as much pains to avoid her as he had been to see her . . . feeling his very heart stop when he did

*T*he reasons are obvious: the decay of religion, increasing moral relativism, the sheer growth of the cities, industrialization, mechanization—all these factors tend to break up the cohesion generated by common background, traditional beliefs, and close personal associations. The relatively tight small-town and farming communities of the older America have been disappearing. But they had certainly not disappeared from the world in which Faulkner grew up, and they have an important place in the world that he created in his fiction.

I, too, grew up in such a world. I took for granted the values I shared with my fellows. It was only years later that I became fully conscious of the beliefs, values, and attitudes that I shared, quite unreflectingly, with others. For such a sense of community is like the air we breathe. One simply takes it for granted. It is only when one is deprived of that air—when one begins to stifle and gasp—that he realizes its importance. Once we have lost our community—and usually not until we have lost it—do we come to value it, or even see it for what it is.

"Faulkner and the Community," an essay by Cleanth Brooks

occasionally see her unmistakable body from a distance. Her white dress in the sun was an unbearable shimmer sloping to her body's motion as she passed from sunlight to shadow. . . leaving him to stare at the empty maw of the house in hope and despair and baffled youthful lust. (Soldier's Pay)

It was World War I, and in his heartbreak he went to Canada and enlisted in the Canadian Royal Air Force. He later wrote and told monumental tales of being a pilot and a warrior. Sometimes, as Mark Twain counseled, you have to lie to tell the truth. When, at twenty-one and the war over, he returned home from Canada, he wore the uniform of a British officer around town, complete with pips, wings of the Royal Flying Corps, Sam Browne belt, cane, and swagger stick. He affected a limp and claimed to have a silver plate in his head from a plane crash. The truth was the war ended before he completed flight training, and he had never shipped out to France.

He had never finished high school. "He simply quit going," his brother John recalled. He enrolled for a time as a special student under veteran's status at the University of Mississippi about a mile from the courthouse square. In these formative years he was a young man of talent struggling to find himself, at war with his surroundings, isolated and tortured by a native genius seeking a means of expression. He began writing self-conscious and pretentious poems and immature stories, and he drew sketches and painted. People of town and gown made fun of him and began calling him "Count No 'Count," an opprobrium that remained with him for many years in the town. He made a D in English and one of the Ole Miss literary societies refused him membership.

Ole Miss has always been small by measure with other state universities, and in 1918 there were fewer than 600 students there; as with the patrician white community of Mississippi then, everyone knew everyone else. There was an affecting intimacy and sophistication to its stunningly beautiful campus in the rolling pastoral woodlands of the Deep South: the antebellum Lyceum at the crest of a hill, the spreading oaks, the huge verdant circles and groves, the bosky languor. Elizabeth Spencer wrote of the Ole Miss of the 1930s, but it could just as easily have been of 1918,

It was a long, twisting drive over narrow, gravel roads to get there in the old days, but once here one immediately felt something distinguished about both town and campus, as though the cultural roots were firm and strong and secure. On the campus, the Lyceum, the observatory, and the grove seemed to have been created to impart a sense of the past, of classical studies, of tradition. Some campuses have this meditative quality and one need know no one ever connected with them to feel it. Others, I believe, never acquire it at all. Ole Miss had it, and Oxford itself had a serene, golden quality all its own.

Ben Wasson, Faulkner's friend at Ole Miss from the remarkably cultured river town of Greenville, later served as his first literary agent, edited the manuscript of *Sartoris*, and helped place *The Sound and the Fury*. Their paths would subsequently cross many times over the years in Hollywood, New York, and Mississippi. Wasson had first been introduced to Faulkner on the Ole Miss campus in 1916 by a somewhat snobbish, philistinistic upper-classman. He recalled his first impressions:

A white handkerchief was tucked in a sleeve of his tweed coat, which seemed curious to me. I thought he looked quite British. His coat had brown leather patches at the elbows, and his baggy trousers were of gray flannel. His brown shoes were highly polished, and his striped tie I later learned was known as a "regimental." He was a bit taller than I and slender. Above his thin lips he wore a smallish moustache that reminded me immediately of Charlie Chaplin's trademark. His nose was aquiline, his eyes dark, piercing and almond-shaped.

"You two fellows should get along fine," the senior student said. "You both like to read poetry and highbrow books. Don't you?"

Faulkner did not reply, and Wasson muttered, "Oh."

"You're a poet, aren't you?" the student said.

"Not John Keats." Faulkner lit a corncob pipe. "Cheerio," he said.

"Is he a college student?" Wasson asked after he had departed.

"He's not a student and don't, so far as anybody knows, do anything. That's why he's called Count No 'Count, I reckon. Lives off his family in Oxford—mother, father, and some brothers, I hear. Plays poker, shoots craps, drinks moonshine whiskey when he can get it. Dabbles in things, they say."

When Faulkner came home from Canada, he and Wasson and brother Murry joined the SAEs, the social fraternity to which Faulkner's father and grandfather had earlier belonged. He and Wasson and other students and townspeople—they called themselves The Bunch—spent many hours at an unprepossessing, two-story wooden-frame café named The Shack opposite the depot, gazing at the passengers in the fashionable passenger trains from Chicago to New Orleans. "We saw flowers on the tables, and incredibly, people were eating and drinking so casually. It was too sophisticated. We wondered where they were going. We longed to go with them."

There was a black man at Ole Miss named Blind Jim. He was a ubiquitous presence on the campus, where he sold peanuts and asked for money, and the unofficial mascot of the athletic teams—"I never saw Ole Miss lose a game," he was known to say. "Bill declared Blind Jim to be a fraud," Wasson remembered, "a conniving character, and a nuisance in whom he placed no belief whatsoever." He judged his "panderings" disgraceful and suggested this to the university authorities, but "Blind Jim was easily more popular among the student body than Bill Faulkner, and...both of them knew it."

He was reading insatiably now, and writing intense lyrical verse patterned mainly after Rimbaud, Verlaine, Housman, Wilde, and the Imagists. A number of his poems appeared at intervals in *The Mississippian*, the student weekly, and his pen-and-ink drawings and poems were published in the yearbook. When its editor told Faulkner he needed a poem "to extol for posterity the beauty and manifold charms of the Ole Miss coed," the fledgling artist complied. The Ole Miss coed, forever lasting! His poem, a sweet, pastoral paean to her in 1919, was ineluctably replaced in 1931 by Temple Drake. This coed ended up in his transmuted mature prose with some highly disreputable characters at the ruin of the Old Frenchman's Place in Yoknapatawpha County and got in serious trouble, in *Sanctuary*, her "taut, toothed coquetry, her high delicate head and her bold painted mouth and soft chin, her eyes blankly right and left looking cool, predatory, and discreet."

"Bill's 'painting pictures' was deemed to be another of his eccentricities," Wasson recalled. "Painting houses or fences, which he did from time to time, was an acceptable task for a man. Painting pictures was odd. Bill wasn't bothered in the least and never would be by what people thought or said about him." He painted skies, trees, unplowed fields, then he would put aside his work and withdraw from his pocket a volume of poems—Yeats, Keats, Shelley—and read aloud. "Poetry's the greatest and most perfect of all the creative arts," he would say. Given these dubious pursuits, Wasson reported, "Bill Faulkner's father thought Bill and I were nuts."

Faulkner's grandfather, who had founded the First National Bank, always wished his eldest grandson to choose banking as a career. ("People keep wondering what William is going to be," he was heard to say. "And all I can say is, he'll either turn out to be a genius or just a plain damned fool.") And for a time in 1918 he worked in that establishment on the courthouse square as a bookkeeper, posting demand debits and demand credits on a daily basis. I find it curiously poignant and touching, his making these arduous

ledger entries he must have hated, nevertheless doing so in his painstakingly neat hand, his delicate, vertical, half-written and half-printed holograph.

It was in the spring of 1921 that he came out with his first book. He "made" it himself, and this, incredibly, less than a decade before *The Sound and the Fury*. He called it *Marionettes*, a one-act play in verse, and he bound it in sturdy cardboard and illustrated it with pen-and-ink line drawings in the Beardsley mode, with a meticulously lettered text.

"Why don't you try to sell it for me to someone?" he asked Ben Wasson.

"How much?"

"You reckon five dollars is too much to ask?"

"I believe I could get it," Wasson said.

"If you sell it, I can make some more books if you'll sell them. I need money right now. Bad."

A little later he ran the university post office, taking the job, of course, because he needed the money and because he could sit in the back for long hours and read and sometimes write poetry. "He was the damnedest postmaster the world has ever seen," a friend said. "It never ceased to amaze us all," his brother Murry recollected. "Here was a man so little attracted to mail that he never read his own, being solemnly appointed as, one might say, the custodian of that belonging to others." A professor filed a bill of complaint that the only way people could get their mail was to dig it out of the trash can at the back door. The postmaster delayed delivery of magazines until he had read them himself. He and his friends played cards in the back and closed down the post office early to go play golf. He seldom put up the mail and people would pound on the doors and scream, "Put up the mail! Put up the mail!" The postmaster paid no attention.

The authorities dispatched a diligent postal inspector who found much of the mail was not only still there but had not even been removed from the bags. He reported that the postmaster "had contrived to foul up a little fourth-class office more completely than some of the best in the business had managed to do with a first-class one." When Bill Faulkner resigned under pressure, he declared that he never again would be at the beck and call of "every S.O.B. who's got two cents for the price of a stamp."

He was also the volunteer scoutmaster for the local Boy Scout troop. He was a fine naturalist. He took the boys on expeditions into the countryside, taught them woodcraft and forestry, told them ghost stories around the campfires, and the boys loved him. Often he would lead them on hikes out to Thacker's Mountain (elevation 623 feet) or into the deepest woods, where they would pitch puptents and sometimes stay a week. Chester McLarty, for years his personal physician and loyal friend, native of the county, Ole Miss and Tulane Medical School graduate, was a boy then and first got to know the scoutmaster when he examined him on various merit badges. "Bill always had a great rapport with children. He didn't stand on ceremony with us. He was very accessible. I never knew a kid he wasn't very good to. And you could tell he truly enjoyed being scoutmaster." But he was later dismissed when a preacher complained about his drinking.

The Fabric of Community

AS HE GRADUALLY CONFRONTED HIS great incipient gifts, was Oxford the town really an incubus on him? At least the people left him alone. His mentor Phil Stone, the hometown lawyer, writing in 1934, thought Oxford in many ways had been "a most favorable field" for the development of his talent. "Nothing is more fatal to the creation of a living and growing art," he said, "than the dead hand of culture." Edith Brown Douds, who grew up near the Falkner family house on the campus and was one of The Bunch with Faulkner and Wasson at The Shack Cafe in the twenties and later knew both Fitzgerald and Hemingway in Paris, agreed. "Much that is written about Faulkner nowadays," she wrote in 1964, "assumes that Oxford was hostile to him and heaped ridicule on him. My recollection, on the other hand, is that he enjoyed, as did we all, a degree of individual freedom which would be difficult to duplicate in most places in the more regimented present-day society." Chester McLarty argues that Bill Faulkner's perception of the town's disdainful view of the Falkner family in the 1920s was considerably worse than it actually was. The father may not have been warmly regarded, but the mother certainly was, and the three younger brothers were attractive and outgoing and gregarious young men.

"Back in the twenties, the word most frequently applied to Bill was *peculiar,*" McLarty recalls, "the peculiar Faulkner boy, the loner, uncommunicative, writes poetry. But Oxford had been a university town since the 1840s. It had known and lived on even terms with many 'eccentrics' before Bill." Walker Percy, a fellow writer and Faulkner's junior, had a more vivid though not dissimilar claim:

I have a theory of why Faulkner became a great writer. It was not the presence of a tradition and all that, as one generally hears, but the absence. Everybody in Oxford, Mississippi, knew who Faulkner was, not because he was a great writer but because he was a local character, a little bitty fellow who put on airs, wore a handkerchief up his sleeve, a ne'er-do-well, Count No-count they called him. He was tagged like a specimen under a bell jar; no matter what he wrote thereafter, however great or wild or strange it was, it was all taken as part of the act. It was part of "what Bill Faulkner did." So I can imagine it became a kind of game with him, with him going to extraordinary lengths in his writing to see if he could shake them out of their mild, pleasant inattention. I don't mean he wanted his fellow Southerners to pay him homage, that his life and happiness depended on what they thought of him. No, it was a kind of game. One can imagine Robinson Crusoe on his island doing amazing acrobatics for his herd of goats, who might look up, dreamily cud chewing for a moment, then go on with their grazing. "That one didn't grab you?" Crusoe might say, then come out with something even more stupendous. But even if he performed the ultimate stunt, the Indian rope trick, where he climbs up a stiff rope and disappears, the goats would see it as no more or less than what this character does under the circumstances. Come to think of it, who would want it otherwise? There is a good deal of talk about community and the lack of it, but one of the nice things about living an obscure life in the South is that people don't come up to you, press your hand and give you soulful looks.

Among many denizens, nonetheless, it indisputably became a habit over the years to observe *him* observing them. Mayor John Leslie—"druggist by trade, mayor by God"—elected in 1973, the same year as the beer referendum (he beat beer by 24 votes), would remember him as often being in a kind of daze. "I don't know how many times I saw him on the square, leaning back against a building, propped up on one leg, just listening to people's conversation. He could spend hours that way. In those days you saw horses and wagons filling the square. He liked particularly to listen to—to talk with—blacks. He was fascinated by their conversation; he had a look when you could tell he was following several conversations at once. I never saw him taking notes, though. I guess he remembered all he needed."

When Leslie was a student at Ole Miss, he approached the writer to sign a copy of *Intruder in the Dust* for his brother who was studying Faulkner's work at Duke University. Faulkner, leaning against the outside wall of a department store, replied, "Well, I've got an agreement with the publisher that I sign a number of books for him and that's all." Leslie thanked him, but turned away disappointed and Faulkner chuckled and said, "Come on, I'll sign that book for you," and did so politely. Later, when he owned his drugstore, Leslie would deliver a package of medicine to Faulkner's mother's house and find him sitting in a green glider on the front porch on South Lamar. "Mr. Leslie, if you have a few minutes, let's pass the time," he would say, and they would talk about what was going on in town, which interested him considerably. M.R. Hall, another courthouse square boulevardier, recalled how the two of them would sit together on a bench with the pigeons all around and talk. Soon he would get up and leave. "I'd wonder about it. And so he'd come back, and I'd say, 'Mr. Faulkner, you kinda slipped off and left me.' He said, 'Yeah, when I think of something I've got to go.' " Louis Cochran, who had known him during their student days at Ole Miss and

later returned to write one of the early pieces on him for the Memphis *Commercial Appeal*, was certain of one thing in the pre-World War I years: "When Bill was to be seen at any hour holding up the posts in front of Rowland's Drugstore or the Bank of Oxford, any bets on the genius side . . . would have found few takers among the citizens. . . . The boot-leggers, the moonshiners, the half-beaten-to-death wives and the half-starved children born without benefit of clergy or resulting from incestuous passion were all around the square. There Bill would stand from early morning until dark, looking them over." Pearline Jones, a much beloved black woman of the town, worked as a maid for his uncle, known to her as "Lawyer" Falkner, and remembers William's visits to the uncle's house. "He was the most straight-backed man in town. Lord, he was the straightest-walking man I ever saw. Sat on the porch just looking out. Never said too much, though. Kind of a *dreamy* man, I'd say."

His fluctuating sartorial proclivities also drew attention. Once an Ole Miss student who admired him followed him into the Oxford post office and observed his attire: he was faultlessly dressed in a sports jacket, bow tie, fine shoes, but he had no socks on. "He could be extremely courtly," his daughter Jill said. "No one could be quite as elegant as Pappy could when he was dressed for the occasion. And you didn't feel embarrassed when he bowed. You could imagine if he had a cloak on he could swing it off and put it in a mud puddle and you could walk on it." One of the graphic memories of Nina Goolsby, editor of the *Oxford Eagle*, of Faulkner on his long walks around town, was fine tweed jackets with leather patches on the elbows and a cane hooked over his arm. The local photographer J.R. Cofield also scrutinized his uncommon whims. "I've seen him uptown in the seediest-looking outfits—old coats that a dog wouldn't lie on. I don't believe he ever threw away a single garment he ever owned." Within hours on the same

day, Cofield would sight him in a proper Madison Avenue outfit, then a genuine Irish linen suit. "And it was nothing to see him immaculately dressed from the waist up, but from the belt down an old pair of khaki farm pants, unpressed and smeared with axle grease."

Some people in town stood by him in his difficult, lonely years—foremost among them the lawyer Phil Stone, one of his early and most valuable advocates, and his mother, Miss Maud.

Phil Stone was four years older than he, an honors graduate of both Ole Miss and Yale, a garrulous man who beginning in about 1916 when Bill Faulkner was twenty, encouraged and counseled the young poet and writer. His law office was a one-story red brick establishment with a turret, not many strides west of the square. Besides being a highly literate and educated man, he knew everything about the county, its past and present, its foibles and failings, and not unlike Faulkner's later character Gavin Stevens, often seemed more interested in gossip than in the thickets of the law. If anyone "discovered" Bill Faulkner, Malcolm Cowley later conceded, it was Phil Stone; in the small-town Oxford of World War I, it was one of the more significant friendships in the history of our American letters. Stone had some of his friend's earlier manuscripts typed in his office and peddled them to various editors, and in 1924 he paid for the printing of *The Marble Faun*. "Wherever Faulkner was he seemed to need someone whom he could call on for various services," the biographer Carvel Collins said, "in addition to the help necessary when drinking had made him ill. Phil Stone, besides being helpful in vastly more important ways, often served also in that mundane supportive role." The Stone house was a white columned antebellum a mile or so out from town, and on one of the window panes there was scratched with a diamond, U.S. Grant 1862. Stone gave Bill Faulkner free run of his library lined deep with the classics and the histories

*T*hrough the long afternoon they clotted about the square and before the jail—the clerks, the idle, the countrymen in overalls; the talk. It went here and there about the town, dying and borning again like a wind or a fire until in the lengthening shadows the country people began to depart in wagons and dusty cars and the townspeople began to move supperward. Then the talk flared again, momentarily revived, to wives and families about supper tables in electrically lighted rooms and in remote hill cabins with kerosene lamps. And on the next day, the slow, pleasant country Sunday while they squatted in their clean shirts and decorated suspenders, with peaceful pipes about country churches or about the shady dooryards of houses where the visiting teams and cars were tethered and parked along the fence and the womenfolks were in the kitchen, getting dinner, they told it again.

From Light in August

and biographies and left him the key to the house whenever he was away. In 1934 Stone wrote a portrait of Faulkner for a short-lived local literary magazine.

It is the likeness of a man who loves his native soil and prefers its people to all others. It is the likeness of a simple-hearted country boy leading the life of a country squire except for the vice of spoiling good white paper with little black marks. It is the likeness of the sanest and most wholesome person I have ever known. It is also the likeness, in the main, of a person most deserving of admiration and respect and friendship in all the walks of everyday life and of a person who, at times and in some small ways, is the most aggravating damned human being the Lord ever put on this earth. Still, and all in all, the true likeness is of a person far and away superior to the great mass of human beings with whom we are all constantly tried—and with whom we try others.

His mother was a tiny wisp of a woman of immense tenacity and pride. "Billy would have had very little," his brother Murry often heard her say, "had he depended on the people of our county for it." "She had an artistic temperament," Chester McLarty remembers. "She was a person of warmth and refinement and consequence." Faulkner's idea of women, of ladies, his daughter Jill says, "always revolved a great deal around Granny [Maud]. She was just a very determined, tiny old lady that Pappy adored. Pappy admired that so much in Granny and he didn't find it in my mother and I don't think he ever found it in anybody. I think that maybe all of these including my mother were just second place." Miss Maud passionately loved literature and passed that on to her sons. She gave them a practicable grasp of English before they entered school, and their rooms were filled with the children's books of the time. The mothers of great artists are often enduring to the history and remembrance of them, and always will be. "She was really touched by what she read," Murry wrote. "I have many times seen her on the verge of tears over one passage, while another would cause her to chuckle in unabashed delight. She never tired of reading the ancient writers—Plato, Aristotle, and the like, but she was just as quick to take up the more current ones." They had a Malay edition of Conrad that eventually became dog-eared with use. She prepared her sons huge breakfasts, and at night she would put a freshly refilled oil lamp on the table in their bedrooms and make them apply themselves to their school lessons. One of her stoutest aversions was of people complaining about their misfortunes; written in neat red paint on a placard hanging over the stove in her kitchen was the admonition, Dont Complain—Dont Explain. Not long after *Sanctuary* was published in 1931, during her weekly rubber of bridge with the ladies of the town, one of them disparagingly mentioned the corncob book. "My Billy writes what he has to," Miss Maud said. She finished the rubber in silence, departed, and never played with that woman again.

Over the years, even after his greatest successes, there were felicitous moments with faithful, non-bookish friends in the town, fellow parents with children and dogs, drinking companions, sometimes revelers.

He and Mr. Mac Reed, of the Gathright-Reed Drugstore on the square, were close friends going back to 1923. "The modesty and shyness of the two men," a mutual acquaintance noted, "created between the two an instant rapport." Whenever Faulkner finished a manuscript he would bring it into the store and Mac Reed would package it and mail it to New York. "Throughout all the years," Reed remembered, "I never knew the proposed title or the suggested title of any story that he ever sent in. During the very early years, of course, Phil Stone handled his manuscripts. Later, Bill would just come in and say, 'Mac, I didn't have anything down at the house to wrap this in. Do you have a box or something?' So we'd go ahead and wrap it and

get it all sealed and ready to go, you know, and he'd have an address label there, and so that would be all there was to it."

Among his best Oxford friends were Ross and Maggie Brown, Hugh and Mary Evans, and Ashford and Minnie Ruth Little. Ross Brown was of the landed gentry, as much a part of Yoknapatawpha in his own way as Faulkner himself, with holdings in the county amounting to some seven or eight thousand acres. He had attended Washington and Lee, and later Ole Miss. His people had come to the town in 1840, three years after its founding, and his uncle John Brown served with Lee; John Brown was in the Lamar Rifles, a sister unit to the University Grays, and was captured at age twenty at the Battle of Falling Waters near Gettysburg, then exchanged, and subsequently came home and was elected mayor of Oxford. For these and other matters there had to have been an affinity between Ross Brown and Faulkner. "They liked each other's company," recollects Brown's son Billy Ross, who likewise would know Faulkner well as a teen-ager in the 1940s. "Both liked to drink whiskey. Dad never read anything Mr. Bill wrote—couldn't understand it," a fact that Faulkner, far from deploring, must have perfervidly appreciated. Colonel Hugh Evans was the commandant of the Army ROTC at Ole Miss, a colorful and flamboyant figure, and Ashford Little was a doctor in Oxford—polished, courtly and a perfect host, his wife Minnie Ruth, a classic Mississippi beauty. The four couples—Faulkners, Browns, Evanses, Littles—frequently were together in the evanescent moments of small-town Oxford.

Of the eight of them, in 1990, only Minnie Ruth Little and Maggie Brown, Ross's widow, remain. "Maggie Brown is fond of all other human beings," a friend once said, "and all other human beings in turn are fond of her." She was of aristocratic lineage from near Vicksburg, a graduate of Ole Miss, a pretty girl of lively and perspicacious disposition. Her great-grandmother had been killed in her own bed by a Union soldier during the Civil War. Once, in the 1950s, Faulkner brought a northern editor to the Browns' house in Oxford for a visit. "Patricia," Faulkner said to the Browns' daughter, "I want you to show my guest the bed back in your bedroom." Maggie Brown recalls, "They went back to the bedroom and stood there for the longest time. Bill pointed to the bullet hole in the headboard and turned to the editor and said, 'This is why the war will never die for these people in the South. This happened in this girl's family.' "

In all the times they were together, Maggie Brown remembers, Bill Faulkner never once talked about his work. "Oh, no! *Never* about writing, not once." And this was in a period that he was writing *Absalom, Absalom!* and *The Unvanquished.* "Bill was one of the sweetest men I ever knew—gentle, thoughtful, fine, loveable. I never heard him saying anything out of the way, or womanizing. If he did that, he didn't do it around here. He was a perfect gentleman, and we were with him a *lot.*" There was a dinner party at the Browns' in the early 1940s with the four couples. "We were getting seated at the table. Ashford Little pulled Mary Evans's chair back a little too far as she was being seated and she hit the floor. Bill immediately pulled his chair back and sat on the floor beside her so she wouldn't be too embarrassed. He was that way."

On another occasion they were in their boat on Sardis Lake. A visiting doctor from Tulane was with them, and he was very drunk. Although it was freezing cold and there were no swimming trunks aboard, the doctor went to the cabin, put on some pajama bottoms, and jumped into the water. Soon he swam back up and said, "I've lost 'em!" and was about to climb in the boat naked. "Bill and Hugh Evans got so furious at the doctor they were red in the face," Maggie remembers. "Bill pushed Mary and me away and put a blanket over the doctor." They had picnics with all their children near a pond

*T*he house didn't seem to get any nearer; it just hung there in front of us, floating and increasing slowly in size, like something in a dream, and I could hear Ringo moaning behind me, and farther back still the shouts and the hoofs. But we reached the house at last; Louvinia was just inside the door, with Father's old hat on her head rag and her mouth open, but we didn't stop. We ran on into the room where Granny was standing beside the righted chair, her hand at her chest.

"We shot him, Granny!" I cried. "We shot the bastud!"

"What?" She looked at me, her face the same color as her hair almost, her spectacles shining against her hair above her forehead. "Bayard Sartoris, what did you say?"

"We killed him, Granny! At the gate! Only there was the whole army, too, and we never saw them, and now they are coming."

From The Unvanquished

out by Taylor, a community six miles from Oxford. The children would have ice-fights and foot races. "Bill would tell stories to the children. Sometimes he'd sing a solo—a song called *Waterboy*. It was a grand way to entertain. We had some good times back then. He loved the children. He loved those times."

In 1938 Ross Brown, Colonel Evans, and Bill Faulkner went on a hunting trip near Port Gibson and returned home with a deer. His wife Estelle could cook venison, and Faulkner organized an elaborate hunt breakfast for a Sunday morning at his house, Rowan Oak. He asked guests to come in costumes. [Of the hunt he would write: "The ancient and unremitting contest according to the ancient and immitigable rules which voided all regrets and brooked no quarter"—and this hunt breakfast was apparently in that spirit.] Maggie Brown remembers Colonel Evans in a Henry VIII costume with a plume in his cap. His wife wore pieces of an old Army uniform. One of the men wore a hunting outfit, and his wife put on his long underwear. Another came in formal riding habit, his wife in a fur cape. Yet another, announcing himself as a knight in mail, arrived with addressed envelopes pinned to his clothes. Faulkner wore jodhpurs, boots, and pink coat. Members of the assemblage met at the Brown house and rode down Second South Street, now South Eleventh, toward Rowan Oak on horses, ponies, and mules. Maggie rode a white mule side-saddle. Since it was a little before eleven on a Sunday morning, the unique caravan, some twenty in number, provoked a Sabbath sensation; for years there was the rumor that a spinster looked out her window and fainted. The assemblage was met at the Faulkner gate by Ned, the longtime retainer, in a mortician's suit; other of the servants wore long black underwear with fezzes on their heads. In greeting, the host, surrounded by barking feists, sounded his hunting horn. The guests were served stirrup cups containing straight shots of Old Forester at fifteen-minute intervals as they paraded around the green grounds. The photographer Cofield, who had been summoned by the host to take some pictures, began to see double images through his camera. Faulkner told the servants, "Pass Cofield up as of right now."

Nine years after this singular event, Faulkner, Brown, Evans, and Little were at a party drinking Canadian Club and conspired to build a houseboat in Colonel Evans's back yard. It would be launched in Sardis reservoir, which had been built by the federal government during the Depression and had the third-largest earthen dam in the world. Billy Ross Brown, Maggie and Ross's son, was thirteen that summer and helped build the boat. "It was one hell of a boat," he remembers: "It took a year of planning," the hull double-planed cypress, each layer corked and nailed with anchor-fast nails, forty-four feet long and fifteen feet wide, with Philippine mahogany panels and a plush galley. Faulkner came to the Colonel's house and worked on it all the time. "He wasn't a very good carpenter, I'll admit," Billy Ross recalls. "He had absolutely no natural ability to nail a nail or saw straight. But he sure the hell tried. Colonel Evans and Mr. Bill would have a fuss about once a day over the details. Mr. Bill would walk home in a huff, but he'd be back the next morning, bright and early." As the boat grew in size it was discovered that a row of cedars in Evans's back yard would have to be cut down to haul the craft to the street. Before dawn one morning when there was sparse traffic, using a tractor to tow it, the freshwater sailors edged their precious cargo through the silent streets of Oxford and around the dark courthouse square, heading out to the lake. They christened the craft *The Minmagary* (an amalgam of Minnie, Maggie, Mary), elected Faulkner skipper and held a launching party at Engineer's Point, Sardis, before a sizeable crowd, the champagne christening being performed by Colonel Evans's wife. The official charter was penned by Faulkner in his tidy script.

By virtue of whatever authority I have inherited from my Great Grandfather William C. Falkner Colonel (paroled) Second Mississippi Infantry Provisional Army Confederate States of America William C. Falkner II reposing all trust & confidence in the staunchness & stability of M/S Minmagary & in the courage & fidelity of her officers and crew do by these presents constitute & appoint her to be a ship of the Line in the Provisional Navy of the Confederate States of America & further direct that all seamen soldiers and civilians recognizing the above authority recognize her as such & accord her all the privileges respect & consideration of that state & condition.

And the accompanying scroll, in part:

M/S MINMAGARY
Oxford

port watch	Hugh Evans, Master	starboard watch
Maggie Brown	Ross Brown, Mate	Minnie Ruth Little
	Ashford Little, M.D., Surgeon	
	Mary Evans, Cabin Boy	

Conceived in a Canadian Club bottle she was born A.D. 15th August 1947 by uproarious Caesarian section in prone position with her bottom upward in Evans' back yard eleven miles from the nearest water deeper than a half-inch kitchen tap and waxed and grew daily there beneath the whole town's rapt cynosure. . . .

And waxed and grew & on the 7th January 1948 rose up and stood on her own bottom to receive the confirmation of her shiphood in deck and superstructure. . . .

In such aspects of the man, a pattern emerges—a man seeking and enjoying on his home soil the company of fine, decent, non-literary people and friends, nothing more nor less. "He was always looking off at the clouds," Maggie Brown remembers. "But what it all was, was humility. He wanted to be one of us."

He went to New Orleans for six months in 1925, where he later claimed he worked for a bootlegger, his principal responsibility being to dig up the whiskey bottles which the sailors from the Bahamas had buried in sandbars and bring them back to the city. He met Sherwood Anderson there and admired his life: writing in the mornings, drinking and walking around in the afternoons. He decided to write a novel there, which became *Soldier's Pay*. Anderson is said to have told him he would send the manuscript to his New York publisher if he did not have to read it.

Taking Anderson's counsel, he finally returned to Oxford, Mississippi, to write his books. It turned out to be a big decision, fraught with consequence. He was frequently broke. It was not easy. He took the odd jobs around the university again and received help from his mother; he painted steeples, dangling precariously high above the ground on ropes, and worked in the Ole Miss power plant. As always he drifted around the town and countryside, got drunk, did not pay his bills. "To them," one of the townspeople remembered, "he was just little Billy Faulkner." Judge John Falkner, when asked by the photographer Cofield if he were any kin to Billy Faulkner, replied, "What, that nut! I'm sorry to say he's my nephew." He told others, "Hell, he ain't ever going to amount to a damn—not a damn." At the time, 1928, the nut was working on *The Sound and the Fury*.

Stranger in a Strange Land

"IF YOU ARE FOOL ENOUGH TO MARRY AT ALL," he wrote Malcolm Cowley years later, "keep the first one and stay as far away from her as much as you can, with the hope of some day outliving her . . . ." In 1929 he married Estelle, who was divorced now and with two children. Ben Wasson described her.

Her body was slim and, like her thin hands, in constant motion. Her eyes were the most vivacious I had ever seen. I couldn't tell you their color, but I know they were animated and sparkling. Her mouth was her least attractive feature, seeming, when pursed up, as it often was, somewhat selfish-looking. She was a lively talker, rarely stopping her chatter, which now and then was mildly malicious. She was flirtatious, a trait she never lost even when she became a much older woman. It was inherent in her nature and was, I'm sure, one of the reasons she was more popular with men than with women. Not that she cared. I suspect she was rather proud of it. She wasn't fond of women.

She was always thoroughly absorbed in whatever a man was saying to her. One would have thought, watching her as she listened to a man, that he was the most fascinating and brilliant creature in the world.

From 1929 to 1932, in this, the most extraordinarily productive period of any American writer in our history, he published *Sartoris*, *The Sound and the Fury*, *As I Lay Dying*, *Sanctuary*, and *Light in August*—all written while he was almost totally ignored as a writer. Not until *Sanctuary* in 1931, which the townspeople called his "corncob book," did his work attract any considerable attention, and even then, owing to the publisher's bankruptcy, he made little money to speak of on the book. Off and on during his life, Faulkner claimed that he had written *Sanctuary* only for the money, which may or may not be true but which detracts gratuitously from this powerful novel. The town's reaction to *Sanctuary* was one of shock, mixed of course with titillation. "People would allude to it," Chester McLarty recalls, "and snicker, like little kids and sex. I'm sure almost all the matrons read it." McLarty found out years later his mother read it in the bathroom. Faulkner's own father, who never read his books, went further. He told people not to buy it. "It's trash," he told his secretary at Ole Miss. "Don't waste your time on it."

The Sound and the Fury, which many consider his most monumental work, or certainly among his two or three greatest, was shrugged off or vilified by most of the national critics. One of their number suggested that the phrase from *Macbeth* used in the title should have been concluded: "signifying nothing." Three thousand copies were printed, and it took sixteen years to sell them. "My brother Bill," Murry wrote, "had a great heart and few people realized, or perhaps cared, how easily he could be hurt." I believe it myth that throughout his life he ignored reviews; my intuition is that he stopped reading them because they hurt. "Bill could only feel bitter," Ben Wasson observed, "that the novel met with such skimpy attention. He later admitted to me that the slight had indeed wounded him and that he believed an author could stand anything more easily than cold indifference." Too, his growing disappointment that the reading public would fail to buy

his books had to have led to bitterness and cynicism about the American "literary" world. He was only human. Several years later, after the publication of *Absalom, Absalom!*, Wasson mustered the courage to ask him how he felt about the harsh critical reception. "I don't know what they said about it," he replied, "but I'm told they didn't like it. But they don't know everything. Someday they'll grow up to that book. It's too much for them." To Wasson the review in *The New Yorker* by Clifton Fadiman, who time and again castigated and made jest of Faulkner's work in the national journals, was "almost hysterically vitriolic." Faulkner wrote a friend: "I did think Fadiman's review was pretty funny. They seem to think I ought to be mad at him. He's got to eat too. I do know, though, Bud, that *Absalom* is the last big one I'll write. It takes too much out of me." On that he proved to be wrong. "Now, many years later," Elizabeth Spencer would write, "we come to his books after a world of critical work at the very highest levels has been accomplished. We can look back on critics, not confined to the South, who misjudged and misunderstood his amazing vision and the variety of his efforts in fiction to make it all plain." Robert Penn Warren later reflected that the whole world was now familiar with Faulkner's voice, but that he could recall the times when for many Southerners like himself "that voice was recognized as an echo of their own previously unformulated experiences." Faulkner, he said, cast a true light on his own Southernness.

I remember how at one time I was outraged by those "outsiders," those Northern reviewers who couldn't see the truth of Faulkner's works. They talked about Southern degeneracy, diseased imagination and Southern fascism.

My outrage at those outsiders was only surpassed by the accounts of certain insiders, those Southerners who complained that Faulkner was a household traitor and the local chamber of commerce really should do something about him.

Yet the early thirties were a mellow time for him personally. To some he seemed almost happy and contented, "the two emotional states," Ben Wasson recalled, "which he most longed for and which thereafter he knew so seldom." In the fall of 1931 he attended a writer's conference at the University of Virginia, where he was overheard gently crooning "Carry Me Back to Old Virginny" in a car in Charlottesville. Though pressed as usual for money, the sale of *Sanctuary* helped, and matters were better than before. He bought a house in Oxford; his daughter Jill was born. His accumulating work was praised by the English critic Arnold Bennett, and Alexander Woollcott touted *Sanctuary* on his "Town Crier" radio show. Louis Cochran described him in the Memphis *Commercial Appeal* after *Sanctuary* was published:

In personal appearance the author is unobtrusive. Of slender height, not over five feet seven, he has the delicate step and waist line of a girl. His eyes are a soft, luminous brown; his hair, darkly of the same tint, is thick and more often tousled than otherwise. A thin face, wide forehead and high cheek bones complete a countenance that is at once remotely aloof and sensitive to every living thing. His voice is low and pleasing to hear; a drawling, soft voice which one could not imagine uttering the gusty epithets of the characters so blindly and ruthlessly trampling across the pages of the author's novels. And yet perhaps it could. . . .

On a trip to New York to meet with publishers, he moved into the Algonquin. Some of the literati wanted to meet him, and Ben Wasson introduced him to them. He wrote Estelle an affecting letter, written not by an exuberant adolescent but by a mature man in his middle thirties. Who among us would have reacted otherwise?

I have created quite a sensation. I have had luncheons in my honor by magazine editors every day for a week now, besides evening parties, or people who want to see what I look like. In fact, I have learned with astonishment that I am now the most important figure in American letters. That is, I have the best future. Even Sinclair Lewis and Dreiser make engagements to see me and Mencken is coming all the way up from Baltimore to see me on Wednesday. I'm glad I'm level-headed, not very vain. But I don't think it has gone to my head.

Dining at the Algonquin he observed from a distance the noted habitués of the Round Table, and thought they were "showing off." One day he and Wasson were strolling past the Scribner's book store on Fifth Avenue and saw a window display of books about a dead writer. "They'll be picking my bones one of these days," he said. "I'd better watch what I do or say from now on, hadn't I?" He enjoyed the time he spent with Frank Sullivan, Marc Connolly, Corey Ford, and Dorothy Parker. "She's one tough lady, ain't she?" is the way he described Parker. He was often in the company of Lillian Hellman and Dashiel Hammett, whom he particularly liked, a fellow American writer of unideological persuasion, a warm and humorous companion with a similar disposition about people and things, a loyal, funny, shy, intelligent man; they frequented the speakeasies where Faulkner once engaged in a long and amiable discussion with a mobster. At one large party he met Bing Crosby. Later, as he and Wasson drove down Broadway, they passed the Paramount Theater with the big twinkling sign "Bing Crosby and His Band" on the marquee. "Was that the same little man I just met, Bing Crosby?" he asked.

Wasson considered it politic for Bill to meet the influential and acerbic Alexander Woollcott, known as the "New Jersey Nero." Faulkner, with some reluctance, went to his rooms in the Barclay Hotel, where the great man, surrounded by hovering admirers and sycophants, lounged on a sofa in a crimson dressing gown. "So, it's Master Faulkner, not looking in the least

*N*ow, riding northward toward New York on the two-lane roads of 1931, he was in no such protective environment. He was with one old friend and two new ones who admired him and would do what they could—like others in New York. For a period of nearly seven weeks Faulkner would be away from home—still grieving for his baby, concerned over his wife's health, worried about money, and engulfed periodically in situations involving tension and crowds.

From Faulkner: A Biography *by Joseph Blotner*

bit sinister," he said to his Mississippi visitor. "I observe you don't have your corncob with you." Faulkner was grimly silent. Woollcott turned to Wasson and inquired how much Negro blood he had in his veins. Then, again to the writer, "You disappoint me, young Massa. You seem much too harmless to have written that horror book. Now, tell me, is Missy Temple a typical Southern belle?" That was it for Bill Faulkner. He swiftly turned around and left the apartment. From the elevator Wasson followed him outside to the street, where Faulkner stopped so quickly that his companion nearly ran into him. He said, "I'd prefer to keep company with Frankenstein's monster."

Not long after this, with Hollywood earnings, he bought an airplane. It was a Waco Cabin bi-plane, known as "the Cadillac of the air," a popular aircraft of the time, with red exterior and brown leather interior and bucket seats and a 210-horsepower Continental engine. He had not flown a plane since Canada in World War I, and he went to Memphis and took lessons all over again from the flamboyant "Captain" Vernon Omlie, who had a flying school there. The Waco Aircraft Company published a journal, *The Waco Pilot*, and in one of its issues it ran a photograph of Bill Faulkner in front of his plane, the new owner tacitly allowing them to propagate the fiction of his having been a veteran World War I combat pilot.

His brother Murry, who likewise became a licensed pilot along with John and Dean, frequently went back and forth with him between Oxford and Memphis. "He was all pilot; his head never moved an inch until we approached the Memphis airport and he turned and shouted to me above the roar of the motor to be sure that my seat belt was fastened. . . . What everlasting pleasure we had flying or just sitting about the airport, looking at airplanes and talking about them." The purchase of the Waco was something Faulkner would one day deeply lament.

Running out of money again, his subsequent books total financial failures, he was forced to spend months at a time writing scripts in Hollywood, often miserably homesick. There was more money in Hollywood, he said, than in all of Mississippi. "I reckon I'll have to go back to Hollywood again," he later told Murry. "The more you make of that damn money, the more you have to make. Instead of being better off with that outrageous money they pay you, you become worse off." He drank heavily in Hollywood, even by his own admission. Once Shelby Foote, whom Stanley Kubrick had wanted to come out to Hollywood and write a script, asked Faulkner's counsel. "Go if you want to," he said, "but let me give you a piece of advice. If you go, never take the people seriously. Hollywood is the only place where you can get stabbed in the back while you're climbing a ladder." He sometimes recounted the story—another myth—that he asked the studio's permission to go home to work on a script, and when they gave it he went home, not to Beverly Hills, but to Mississippi.

"One day a leaf falls in a canyon out there," he said, "and they call it winter." He would likely have agreed with Truman Capote's later assessment of the Hollywood *milieu*: no children, no dogs, no cracks in the sidewalks. The Hollywood stars, basking in the bright lights of the studio system, the fabulous glamor crowd, held not the faintest interest for him, although he did meet some of them, such as Claudette Colbert, ZaSu Pitts and Clark Gable. Fragments of Hollywood talk:

"My husband and I admire your books very much," Claudette Colbert said.

"Thank you, ma'am. And I liked you in that picture with Clark Gable. I've met him."

"Clark's a great guy, and no foolishness about him. Fine to work with, too. Not temperamental at all."

"I don't know the movie stars, just writers that write the movies for the actors' and actresses' benefit."

Leaving the premises with Ben Wasson, he said, "Miss Claudette's legs are better when you really see them than they are on a movie screen, ain't they?"

Strolling along a tennis court with ZaSu Pitts:

"I love to read, but I'm not a very literary person," she said.

"Thank God for that. Not too long ago I was at a literary convention in Charlottesville, Virginia. God save us from that."

The director Howard Hawks, for whom he was writing a script, recalled the day he introduced him to Gable.

Faulkner and I were going hunting down in Imperial Valley after doves, and Clark Gable called up and said, "What are you doing?" I said, "We're going hunting. I'm going hunting with a fella called Bill Faulkner." And he said, "Can I go?" I said, "Yeah, if you can get over here in half an hour." So he came charging over, and we got in the station wagon. We had a couple of drinks on the way down. We started talking, and I don't know what, the conversation got into literature and Gable said, "Who do you think are the good writers, Mr. Faulkner?" Faulkner says, "Thomas Mann, Willa Cather, John Dos Passos, Ernest Hemingway, and myself." And Gable looked kinda funny and said, "Do you write, Mr. Faulkner?" Faulkner says, "Yes, what do you do, Mr. Gable?"

There were ups and downs. He spent pleasant hours at Stanley Rose's bookstore on Hollywood Boulevard with Nathaniel West, John O'Hara, Budd Schulberg, and Dashiel Hammett, with whom he renewed their Manhattan friendship; he went pig-hunting on an island off the coast with West. And he had a girlfriend there named Meta Wilde, tall and good-looking, whom he enthusiastically introduced to Ben Wasson, later telling

him he was in love with her—could not get her out of his mind or system.

"She's certainly attractive," Wasson said.

"She was brought up in Mississippi," he said. ("As if that," Wasson later surmised, "explained everything.")

He wrote scripts for bad movies, and for good ones—Raymond Chandler's *The Big Sleep*, Hemingway's *To Have and Have Not*—but I myself have learned there may be no two more disparate places in all of America than Hollywood and Mississippi, which exist so differently in the Great Republic as to be nearly untranslatable one to the other: the unmitigatingly tragic, memory-obsessed Mississippi earth on the one hand, the bland mitigating boulevards and fashionable Beverly Hills cul-de-sacs on the other, with the twinkling, deracinated Hollywood vistas below, and the corrugated tableaux of popular tinsel dreamland. Yet he bravely wrote much of *Absalom, Absalom!* there, pecking away with two fingers on a small typewriter at an upstairs desk in Wasson's house on Sweetzer Street, one of four small "Alpine" chateaus a block away from Sunset Towers. "It's a tortured story," he said one day to Wasson, "and a torture to write it."

Enmity persisted in his hometown. Shelby Foote, then a student at Chapel Hill, recalls driving unannounced into Oxford in the late 1930s to try to find him. He parked his car at the courthouse and asked a man sitting on a bench for directions to William Faulkner's house. The man looked at him, then turned his head and spat on the ground in disgust.

With Foote on this day was his contemporary from Greenville, Mississippi, also a Chapel Hill undergraduate, Walker Percy. But Percy was a shy young man of sixteen and did not go into Faulkner's house with his friend: "I'm not going in there and bother that man." Foote said Mr. Faulkner was a writer. "It's all right, we'll go see him." And Percy: "Well, you can go knock

on his door. I'm not going to do it." He stayed in the car and read a book, although later regretting he did not go. There is something fine in this picture, and satisfying: two Mississippi teenagers, destined someday to be distinguished American writers themselves, among the best, sitting in their car debating whether to knock on William Faulkner's front door in Oxford, Mississippi. Foote did knock on the door, which Faulkner opened, and the young stranger ended up spending two hours with him. It was the first of many visits, and Foote found his host different from the conception of him as a secretive, standoffish man. "He was outgoing, friendly, almost cavalier in manner and very glad to talk about his work, once he was convinced you weren't trying to pry into his private life, which I certainly wasn't. And a congenial companion. . . . He seemed like William Faulkner to me, man and writer. I didn't find any gap between the two. He was a friendly, even outgoing man with certain reticences. His reticence never bothered me; I figured a man with that big a genius strapped to his back would be bound to have some pretty hard times. I'm sure that's nearly always true of great writers. I simply liked him. He was a good companion, a likeable man, a great deal of humor, a gracious host, and seemed like a fine husband—which I later found out he was not. But I liked him."

Even when they did not read him, the townspeople then naturally wondered if they were characters in his books, particularly Snopeses. "Somebody said I was a genius writer," he once told a companion. "The only thing I'd claim genius for is thinking up the name *Snopes*." One day in Hollywood, apropos of nothing at all, he walked up to a screenwriter, David Hempstead, and said, "You know the Snopeses ship 'em to each other." Hempstead asked, "Ship what, Bill?" He said, "Other Snopeses. They just walk down to the station and they put an address card around their neck or stamp it into their lapel and mail 'em to the next town to another Snopes, and

that's the way they're all over Mississippi, all Snopeses shippin' Snopeses to other Snopeses."

In the Yoknapatawpha saga, he contrasts the rapacious greed of these poor whites, many of them descendants of Civil War bushwhackers and villainous thieves, with the wariness of the yeoman farmers and the decadence of the fallen aristocrats. The Old South was eventually plundered and corrupted from within by a coalition of Yankee commerce and the Snopeses, with all that that entailed. Around the turn of the century Flem Snopes, the first one, arrived in Frenchman's Bend, several miles to the southeast of Faulkner's fictional county seat, Jefferson, gained control of that somnolent little hamlet, and when this was accomplished, the clan began to descend on Jefferson itself. So that by the beginning of the twentieth century, he wrote of the mythical town, Snopeses were everywhere.

. . . not only behind the counters of grubby little side street stores patronized mostly by Negroes, but behind the presidents' desks of banks and the directors' tables of wholesale grocery corporations and in the deaconries of Baptist churches, buying up the decayed Georgian houses and chopping them into apartments and on their death-beds decreeing annexes and baptismal fonts to the churches as mementos to themselves or maybe out of simple terror.

This took in a precariously broad swathe, and still does today. Not too long ago in the real Oxford, in fact, a few businessmen and bankers needed a name for a corporation they had formed which was to be listed on the Chicago Commodities Exchange. They arrived at The Flem Snopes Corporation. Sadly, the Snopes Corporation went defunct.

There were rumors around town that he did not write the books (bringing to mind the old saw, attributed to Mark Twain, that Shakespeare

did not write the plays, just some fellow with the same name). For a long time one gentleman of the town argued before anyone who cared to listen that the books were written by an erudite farmer who preferred not to sign his name, and that Bill Faulkner did not know the meaning of all the big words. Evans Harrington, for years the chairman of the English Department at Ole Miss, remembers going to the parcel service to send a manuscript to New York. "You write books?" a parcel clerk asked. Harrington admitted that he did. "William Faulkner writes books," the man said. "At least he says he does. Phil Stone really writes his books for him. At least he puts the punctuation in. I hear Faulkner's movin' to Virginia. We'll see *now* who writes those books."

Even as recently as the early 1950s, after Faulkner had won the Nobel Prize for Literature, when Evans Harrington was teaching English in the local high school, his students exchanged snickers and knowing glances when he assigned them the short story, "A Rose for Emily." He asked them to explain their reactions. "We know about him," one of them said. "He's just an old drunk." They told Harrington of the delivery boy who claimed to have gone to Faulkner's house and seen him naked in a cedar tree. Other tales had both Faulkner and his wife Estelle naked on the lawn or in various trees.

If the years from 1929 to 1942 were his most productive, in the 1940s he was decidedly at his lowest ebb. In the United States all but one of his books were out of print. He was unread, unbought, unrespected. For a man with chronic money problems, by World War II his fortunes were at their nadir. He had unpaid bills all over Oxford. He took out a notice in the *Oxford Eagle* disclaiming any debts incurred by Estelle; even to this most maverick of men, this must have been an appalling humiliation. For an honest writer to make a living in the South, he said, was "like a man trying to make an Egyptian water wheel in a Bessemer foundry."

A local merchant, Will Lewis of the J.E. Neilson Company, attempting to collect overdue bills, asked Faulkner to sign some checks in order to provide monthly payments spread out over some months. Faulkner wrote him back.

J.E. Lewison Co., *Oxford, Miss.*
City. *31 January, 1941*

Dear Will:

I'm not going to sign these checks anymore than I ever signed the checks and notes you have filled out and sent to me in the past. Attached is my own check for ten. I will send more on the account when I can. I make no promise as to when that will be.

I tried last summer to explain to you about $1600.00 additional 1937 income tax which I was trying to pay, two years after my Hollywood income had ceased and when for two years my income had been reduced about 95%, but naturally I did not expect you to listen to it much, since J.E. Neilson cant be anymore interested in Wm Faulkner's hard luck stories than Wm Faulkner can be interested in J.E. Neilson's. But that's the situation. I am trying now to meet the last $853.00 payment, for which demand (also with threats) was made Dec. 20. So if I were going to give anyone a series of signed checks, I would give them to the grocers and fuel people who in their kindness have supplied myself and my dependents with food and heat during this time, and to whom I owe a lot more than even Estelle et al managed to get into you for.

If this dont suit you, the only alternative I can think of is, in the old Miltonic phrase, sue and be damned. If you decide on that step, be assured that I shall do my best to see that the people who have fed me and my family will be protected, and after Uncle Sam gets through with his meat-cutting, J.E. Neilson can have what is left. You may even get an autographed book. That will be worth a damn sight more than my autograph on a check dated ten months from now.

Wm Faulkner

*T*he hum of their voices and movements came back upon the steady draft which blew through the door. The air entered the open windows and blew over the heads and back to Horace in the door, laden with smells of tobacco and stale sweat and the earth and with that unmistakable odor of courtrooms; that musty odor of spent lusts and greeds and bickerings and bitterness, and withal a certain clumsy stability in lieu of anything better. The windows gave upon balconies close under the arched porticoes. The breeze drew through them, bearing the chirp and coo of sparrows and pigeons that nested in the eaves, and now and then the sound of a motor horn from the square below, rising out of and sinking back into a hollow rumble of feet in the corridor below and on the stairs.

From Sanctuary

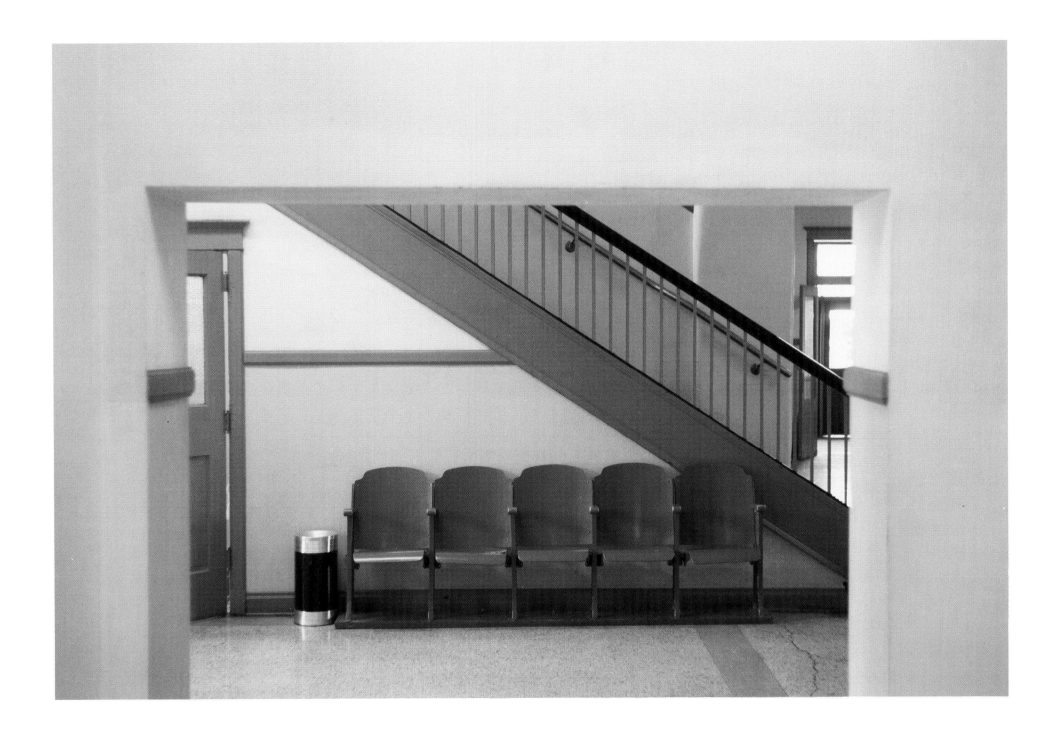

70

In May, 1940, he wrote Robert K. Haas:

Beginning at the age of thirty I, an artist, a sincere one and of the first class, who should be free even of his own economic responsibilities and with no moral conscience at all, began to become the sole provider, principal and partial support—food, shelter, heat, clothes, medicine, kotex, school fees, toilet paper and picture shows—of my mother, my brother's wife and children, another brother's widow and child, a wife of my own and two step children, my own child; I inherited my father's debts and his dependents, white and black without inheriting yet from anyone one inch of land or one stick of furniture or one cent of money . . . I am 42 years old and have already paid for four funerals and will certainly pay for one more and in all likelihood two more besides that, provided none of the people in mine or my wife's family my superior in age outlive me before I ever come to my own.

In such times he would have agreed with his fellow writer Walker Percy about writing in America: "It's a strange, abject, little-understood profession."

Malcolm Cowley, the distinguished literary critic, had started reading and re-reading Faulkner's works. He was appalled by the lack of regard and attention they had received in America. In 1942 the War Resources Committee asked publishing houses to sacrifice their linotype plates because of the copper shortage; Random House junked the plates of its Faulkner books. With all the others out of print, Cowley recalled, "It was just as if somebody had taken a wet cloth and wiped out the blackboard." Cowley was to publish the *Viking Portable Hemingway* in 1944. The Viking Portables presented in individual volumes to a wide readership a representative selection from the works of outstanding writers, each prefaced by a lengthy critical essay. They "have done more for good reading and good writers than anything that has come along since I can remember," Arthur Mizener wrote. About this time Cowley began corresponding with Faulkner about a

series of articles on him for national publications, which later would grow into a *Portable Faulkner*, to include stories and episodes forming a history of life in metaphorical Yoknapatawpha. (Cowley's *Viking Portable* was published in 1946 and had a stunning and salubrious effect on Faulkner's reputation in America. It would subsequently go through fifteen printings.)

Cowley first wrote him in 1944 asking about his life history and his work. Three months passed before he received a reply postmarked Hollywood:

Dear Mr. Cowley: I have just found your letter by idle chance today. . . . My mail consists of two sorts: from people who dont write asking me for something, usually money, which, being a serious writer trying to be an artist, I naturally dont have, and from people who do write, telling me I cant. . . . I dump the letters into a desk drawer, to be read when (usually twice a year) the drawer overflows.

Cowley attempted to sell his first article about Faulkner to national magazines before actually writing it. He tried *The Atlantic Monthly* while he was in Boston, "and the net result was a lunch at the Bulldog Club. Lobster, sherry, old fashioneds, two bottles of Bordeaux and some very old Rhine. The *Atlantic* turned thumbs down. Thumbs a little greasy with lobster dipped in butter."

In the course of this correspondence Cowley, perhaps sensing Faulkner's sagging spirits, wrote him encouraging letters. The French at that time were discovering his books in the fine translations of Maurice Coindreau; from the outset France appreciated them more than his native land. Sartre, Camus, and Robbe-Grillet became nearly reverential; in wartime France under Nazi oppression, his works of Yoknapatawpha County, Mississippi, had special relevance to global suffering and tragedy: Faulkner's Mississippi related to collaborationist France. "Did I tell you what Jean Paul Sartre said about your

work?" Cowley wrote him in 1945. "He is the best of the new French dramatists." He says that his work is based on what he learned from American literature. What he said about you was, 'Pour les jeunes en France, Faulkner c'est un dieu.' " (For the young people in France, Faulkner is a god.) In another letter he gave him "a New York market report on your standing as a literary figure."

Very funny and a credit to you. First, in publishing circles, your name is mud. They're all convinced that your books won't ever sell. "It's a pity, isn't it?" they say with a sort of pleased look on their faces. Second-rate bright boys among the critics do a swell job of incomprehending and underselling you. Fadiman especially. Now, when you talk to writers instead of publishers . . . it's quite a different story. There you hear almost nothing but admiration. The better the writer, the greater the admiration is likely to be. Conrad Aiken, for example, puts you at the top of the heap. The funny thing is the academic and near academic critics and the way they misunderstand and mistake your works.

In these years in his own home town, his brother John remembered, the Ole Miss faculty considered awarding him an honorary degree, but the proposal was voted down. After he got the Nobel Prize, the academics of the University of Mississippi who previously voted against him brought him up again. The others said, "For shame. We can't afford to give him one now. It's too late."

Mississippi was a place that had played out the richest and darkest passions of our nation. It was the poorest state in America, and with the largest black population—histrionic, inward, and given to bleak, self-destructive extremes. W.H. Auden wrote of Yeats: "Mad Ireland hurt you into poetry." There was similarity between Mississippi and Ireland, between Faulkner and Yeats.

Yet, in spite of rejection, Faulkner loved Mississippi. "It's my country, my native land," he wrote. "You don't love because: you love despite; not for the virtues, but despite the faults." And he loved Oxford. "I've lived here all my life and any time I've been away, I've come back as soon as possible." When Hollywood wished to buy the rights to *Light in August*, he said he would charge them $300,000 if they filmed it there, but only $150,000 if it was done in Mississippi.

"It's a shame he wasn't appreciated more at home in his prime," Richard Howorth, owner of Square Books, across from the courthouse, says today, "but then it's a shame he wasn't appreciated more elsewhere. It wasn't Oxford's fault that all his books were out of print in 1945. People didn't know what he was doing, but that would've been the case in small towns all over America then—and now, too."

Mississippi's attitude toward him in those years of his most fruitful work, and also later, was that of his home town writ large. The liberal Delta editor Hodding Carter, Jr., stated that Faulkner was a "pariah" to white Mississippians, "whom he knew better than they knew themselves and pitied and loved." Elizabeth Spencer recalls Mississippians judging him flashy and without substance, "trying to drag our culture through the dirt, to degrade and make fun of our ideals." People told her they would not have a book of his in their house. "Here was a man, one of us right over here at Oxford, shocking us and exposing us to people everywhere with story after story, drawn from the South's own private skeleton closet . . . the hushed-up family secret, the nice girl who wound up in the Memphis whorehouse, the suicides, the idiot brother kept at home, the miserable poverty and ignorance of the poor whites . . . the revenge shootings, the occasional lynchings, the real life of the blacks. What was this man trying to do?"

From my own boyhood in Mississippi in the late 1940s and early 1950s

I recall being told that he was "out for the Yankee dollar," the most pejorative of indictments in that day. "He's crazy," one man in my town said. "Have you tried to read that gibberish? He gets naked and climbs trees." When I was twenty-one, I found myself defending him in a Rhodes Scholarship interview. The chairman of the committee, a wealthy and prominent businessman, replied that if it were up to him, he would have Faulkner run out of the state. The librarian at Blue Mountain College in northeast Mississippi kept all of Faulkner's books under lock and key in a cabinet in her office and refused to catalogue them, only allowing a few students she deemed "mature enough" to read them. (And it was not just in Mississippi. In 1948 in Philadelphia, Pennsylvania, the chief inspector of the vice squad raided bookstores without a warrant and seized *Mosquitoes*, *Sanctuary*, and *The Wild Palms*, among other books. In 1954 the National Organization of Decent Literature placed three of his novels on the disapproval list, which were likewise condemned by many local censorship groups around the country. In Graves County, Kentucky, as recently as 1986, the Board of Education banned *As I Lay Dying* for the schools because it dealt in "reincarnation.")

Most Mississippi editors and journalists wrote virulently of him over the years, calling him a traitor, a renegade, a pornographer, and in numerous instances a Communist. One Mississippi journalist wrote: "Mr. Faulkner's desire for money has . . . led him to writing of unnatural rape and the stink of bodies long dead but unburied." The most widely read columnist in the state, one Fred Sullens of the *Daily News* in Jackson, the capital city, vied with

the Yankee Clifton Fadiman in calumny and ridicule. Here is a typical Mississippi editorial in 1949:

The "Deep South Mayhem" school of literature has become the biggest money-maker for New York publishers. Land below the Mason-Dixon Line is presented as peopled with decadents, degenerates, perverts, half-wits and poltroons by authors indigenous to the South. . . .

The father of this school of Southern defamation is William Faulkner. His thousands of disciples, with nothing to recommend them but possession of a typewriter and some slight knowledge of Freud, make the whole region look like a "Snakepit." Now he has been awarded the Nobel Prize for Literature.

The leaders of the South . . . should start a revolt against these propagandists of degradation. The United Nations might use the UNESCO to protest.

Of a piece with the state's castigation of its native son was the persistent *national* attitude toward Mississippi as the most savage and backward of all the American commonwealths. When the ubiquitous and immortal Fadiman was once asked if he thought Faulkner was ever influenced by Dante's *Divine Comedy*, he replied, "No, because I don't think anyone down there has ever read Dante's *Divine Comedy*." As a student in Oxford, England, in 1957, I had occasion to meet and talk with Robert Frost. He asked me where I was from, and when I said Mississippi, he said, "That's the worst state in the Union." I replied that it had produced good writers. "Can't anyone down there read them," he said.

Yoknapatawpha Revisited

ONE OF THE EARLIEST AND MOST PERsistent misconceptions of Faulkner's work was that he was a "sociologist" reporting the authentic facts of life in Mississippi, and residents of the state continuously deplored his books because they were inaccurate about those facts and contained an insufficient "magnolia quotient." They failed, or did not wish, to see the universality of his message, of his people and places and themes, how he used what he knew to transcend the mere locale and write of "the human heart in conflict with itself . . . the old verities and truths of the heart, the old universal truths lacking which any story is ephemeral and doomed—love and honor and pity and pride and compassion and sacrifice." The mythical Yoknapatawpha County, says the poet James Seay of Panola County, Mississippi, and Chapel Hill, "exists both in and out of time. It is timeless in the way that the landscape and human motion arrested on Keats's Grecian urn are timeless, and in the way that Keats's ode itself—which Faulkner refers to in "The Bear," summoning the same idea—exists out of time." Yet Bill Faulkner did care about what the people of his state thought about him; he knew they were bitter because they thought he gave a fallacious and negative and immediate impression of it. Carvel Collins, the Harvard professor who in 1942 established the first university seminar devoted exclusively to Faulkner, brings us to the crux of the question:

When you think about what Faulkner's purpose was, to draw on the life he knew but to go far beyond it toward the more universal and to do so in this novel by his adaptation of Joyce's mythical method, equating his characters in an inverse way with Demeter and other personages and events of myth. . . I do not feel that we should consider the residents of Mississippi to have been particularly imperceptive, and if the professionals who were making their living by writing criticism did not figure this out, why should civilians be expected to do so? Faulkner more than anyone else, of course, would have been aware of all this . . . and presumably was thinking of it when, having been asked that question whether he thought his novels gave an inaccurate picture of this region, he replied, "Yes, and I'm sorry."

And his biographer, Joseph Blotner:

In my opinion Faulkner is the best novelist that this country has produced. For several reasons: I think he belongs certainly in the company of Hawthorne, Melville, and James because of his technical accomplishments, but also because of the way in which his themes deal with the most important concerns and with the fundamentals of the human condition. Like many writers, he has been called a regionalist. This is not quite fair, it is a limiting term. He represents this country, the Deep South, better than anyone else has ever done—with authenticity, with vividness, with a complete sense of conviction—but at the same time his work carries universal meanings.

After he won the Nobel Prize, he wrote to an Oxford friend. "I fear some of my fellow Mississippians will never forgive that $30,000 that durn foreign country gave me for just sitting on my _____ and writing stuff that makes my own state ashamed to own me."

But as pleased as he surely must have been when Malcolm Cowley, in his 1945 "New York market report," wrote to him about the nearly unqualified adulation of his practicing fellow artists of that day, would he not be equally gratified by the profound and unceasing devotion of his fellow *Mississippi* writers? Tennessee Williams of Columbus began reading him early on and found him a "very, very honest man," linking him with Hemingway and Stephen Crane for the power of his realism. Eudora Welty of Jackson, an early advocate and admirer, as a young woman had a hard time finding his books in the stores in Mississippi, where you could hardly buy them at all, and usually bought them second-hand in New Orleans and other places. "I was just reading his books," she remembers, "because I loved to read them, and not that I could emulate—indeed I never did emulate. Of course as time went on Faulkner became much more accessible and much more widely appreciated in his home state, which took some doing." She recalls how the front-page columnist, Fred Sullens, would lash out at him in the Jackson *Daily News*, and once included her with Faulkner in the Garbage Can School of Literature. "I don't recall why," she says. "He could never have read anything. But he thought we should all be lumped together. He put a whole bunch in there. Faulkner had to contend with that." He once sent her an encouraging note when her book *The Robber Bridegroom* came out and asked if there was anything he could do for her in Hollywood. She was proud of that letter but lent it to a friend, and it turned up not long ago at the University of Virginia, purchased by Jefferson's great Commonwealth for a substantial sum.

Richard Wright of Natchez warmly respected him. Margaret Walker remembers from Wright's younger days that he was "clearly a student of Faulkner and was truly influenced by him." He was "ecstatic" about *Sanctuary* and much taken with *Light in August* and *Absalom, Absalom!* (In this

period, too, the black writers Ralph Ellison and Albert Murray were reading him as students at Tuskegee with equal enthusiasm, and in Nashville, Arna Bontemps told a friend he was reading Faulkner because he was learning how to write and he had not found any writer who could teach him as much.) Faulkner wrote Wright a letter from Hollywood in 1945, which pleased him so much that he had it framed and hung over his desk:

Dear Richard Wright:

I have just read Black Boy. *It needed to be said, and you said it well. Though I am afraid (I am speaking now from the point of view of one who believes that the man who wrote* Native Son *is potentially an artist) it will accomplish little of what it should accomplish, since only they will be moved and grieved by it who already know and grieve over this situation.*

You said it well, as well as it could have been said in this form. Because I think you said it much better in Native Son. *I hope you will keep on saying it, but I hope you will say it as an artist, as in* Native Son. *I think you will agree that the good lasting stuff comes out of one individual's imagination and sensitivity to and comprehension of the suffering of Everyman, Anyman, not out of the memory of his own grief.*

A friend of yours lives in my town, Joe Brown. He has shown me his verse. I have (I hope) helped him to learn what you learned yourself: that to feel and believe is not enough to write from. He has not read enough. He has taken my advice lately. The things he has sent me since I have been here (since June) are improving. I am returning to Oxford, Miss., next week, when I shall see him.

Faulkner's impact on the young Shelby Foote of Greenville was instantaneous. He was a high school freshman in Greenville in 1932, and *Light in August* was one of the first "modern" novels he ever read. "I suppose almost everybody can remember his first modern novel," he recalls, "if he

was lucky enough to read a good one—how different it was from what came before it and how it just knocked you off your feet." Faulkner was showing him his native country, Mississippi, which he thought he knew well, "and showing me how really little I knew it compared to him." Faulkner had a "curious paradoxical approach to things." Foote always sent his books to him; he saw him shortly after sending him his second one. "I liked your book," Faulkner said. "Do better next time."

Elizabeth Spencer of Carrollton began reading him at Vanderbilt. She discovered "how woefully ignorant I was of him." People knew very little about his work at the time, she remembers. "It was a mystery of how the whole pattern of the county was fitted together. This was a great discovery, but I found it very late. Then I began to read everything he wrote. I know that some of his influence got into my work because I was from north Mississippi, so that was all I knew to write about. We were looking at the same things, like Italians painting Madonnas—the same subject occurs over and over and over. I had to find some independence."

To young Ellen Douglas of Greenville, whose father-in-law had been the roommate of Estelle Faulkner's first husband at Ole Miss, Faulkner's words struck her not only with their vigor and overwhelmingly hypnotic style, "but in the sense that he was a writer who was *here*. You recognized that what he had done and what he was doing was something that was needed—and possible—in your own society, and that you might be able to do that kind of thing yourself. It might have seemed very far away from you—unreal—if you had grown up in Iowa. Of course he was in Oxford when I was at Ole Miss, and the great books were coming in those years."

Richard Ford of Jackson recalls that by the time he began writing fiction after high school "it was already impossible to think of Mississippi—its landscapes, its races, its dreams, its fears—except in the terms Faulkner had

All the men in the village worked in the mill or for it. It was cutting pine. It had been there seven years and in seven years more it would destroy all the timber within its reach. Then some of the machinery and most of the men who ran it and existed because of and for it would be loaded onto freight cars and moved away. But some of the machinery would be left, since new pieces could always be bought on the installment plan—gaunt, staring, motionless wheels rising from mounds of brick rubble and ragged weeds with a quality profoundly astonishing, and gutted boilers lifting their rusting and unsmoking stacks with an air stubborn, baffled and bemused upon a stumppocked scene of profound and peaceful desolation, unplowed, untilled, gutting slowing into red and choked ravines beneath the long quiet rains of autumn and the galloping fury of vernal equinoxes.

From Light in August

already given us. It was an incursion on my imagination before I had a chance. Writing is almost always an act of desperation. All I could do was to leave, try to find another place I could imagine anew and for myself."

Barry Hannah of Clinton likewise began reading him early on; he was impressed how his work "made the ordinary move with a suspension and speed at the same time, even in the way Joyce couldn't do. He said he didn't care for music aloud. No wonder. There was an orchestra and symphony and jazz band at the same time in his mind, and this was true for his characters, even the shade-tree mechanics. He was always proving to me the little man means a lot."

Will Campbell of East Fork in Amite County began reading him in the 1940s at Wake Forest and was overcome by "the sheer beauty of the language and what he could do with words. I was envious of that, and a little intimidated." He and a friend would read Faulkner together and merely for the fun of it compose Faulkner-like paragraphs. "Later, when I did turn to writing," Brother Will recalls, "I'd try hard not to write like Faulkner, yet I'd have been happy if I could."

James Whitehead of Jackson read a few of his short stories as a student at Jackson Central High, but it was in the late 1950s in college that he got into the novels. "He made sense for me out of where I was living. It was a kind of relief to find somebody who understood what was happening. He's our great writer." At age eighteen, in 1958, Whitehead and two young Mississippi friends, one of whom, a country boy from Panola County, wanted to talk about dogs with Mr. Bill Faulkner, drove to Oxford and went unannounced to his house just as Foote and Percy had done. He was standing alone in the cedar-lined driveway. "Oh my God," Whitehead whispered to his companions, "there he is!" They approached him. "What do you want?" Faulkner asked. "We'd like to talk to you, sir." They ended up sitting on the front gallery for about forty-five minutes. "It was easy with him," Jim Whitehead remembers, "and graceful and fun." Bill Faulkner smoked his pipe and discussed with the youngsters Russian novelists, Dickens, and dogs, and at his invitation they were about to help him cut some hay behind the house just before a violent summer rainstorm descended.

Ellen Gilchrist of Vicksburg was introduced to his work by none other than Eudora Welty in one of Miss Welty's writing classes at Millsaps College in Jackson in 1962. Miss Gilchrist was twenty-seven years old then, with three children, and thought she might want to be a writer someday. The story Eudora Welty gave her to read was "The Bear." "I'd been told all along growing up in Mississippi that William Faulkner was a traitor." A belligerently anti-Faulkner newspaper editor of her mother's generation warned her not to read him, charging that Faulkner was a plagiarist. She asked whom he plagiarized. "Shakespeare and the Bible," the editor replied.

For Walker Percy of Greenville, Faulkner was "at once the blessing and curse of all Southern novelists, maybe all novelists." Percy, who majored in chemistry in college and whose education until the age of thirty was almost entirely scientific, read *The Sound and the Fury* in high school. When he arrived as a freshman at Chapel Hill, he took the qualifying placement test in English, with classes divided, as Percy remembers, into "advanced, average, and retarded." He wrote the placement theme in a Faulknerian style. "I wrote one long paragraph without punctuation. They put me in the retarded English class, and the professor really thought I was hot stuff. Compared to the rest of the dummies I guess I was."

To Faulkner poetry was the highest art form, and he always called himself a failed poet. "The poets are wrong of course . . . but then, poets are almost always wrong about the facts. That's because they are not interested in facts:

only in truth, which is why the truth they speak is so true that even those who hate poets by simple natural instinct are exalted and terrified by it." He was a passionate craftsman. "That's all any story is. You catch this fluidity which is human life and you focus a light on it and you stop it long enough for people to be able to see it." While he was writing *Absalom, Absalom!* in Hollywood and Ben Wasson asked how it was progressing, he said, "It moves along. Word by word. Sentence by sentence, page by page, and then one day a book's finished. Ain't any book easy to write. Lots simpler to make a coffin." He described the writing of *The Sound and the Fury*, surely his most complex and convoluted mosaic with the monumental shifting of his characters in time, old remembered time at one with the present, as "almost like trying to write the Lord's Prayer on the head of a pin." In "The Bear" one sentence alone occupies 1,800 words, and in the middle of it is a two-page parenthesis, each of the paragraphs beginning with an uncapitalized letter. He baffled even sophisticated readers with these circuitous modes; he knew it. "I'm telling the same story over and over to myself and the world," he wrote Cowley. "I am trying to go a step further."

This, I think accounts for what people call the obscurity, the involved form of style, the endlessentences. I'm trying to say it all in one sentence with one capital and one period. I'm still trying to put it all, if possible, on one pinhead . . . I don't know how to do it. All I know to do is to keep on trying in a new way.

He enjoyed shrouding himself in the enigma of his calling. A bordello was the best place for a writer to live because the mornings were quiet and there was social activity in the evenings and the madame, girls, and police called you "Sir," and you needed nothing more than bourbon and cigarettes, and pencils and paper. He went to lengths to tell reporters and scholars that he was really just a Mississippi farmer. "I don't know any literary people," he would say. "The people I know are other farmers and horse people and hunters, and we talk about horses and dogs and guns and what to do about this hay crop or this cotton crop, not about literature." He wrote about the South, he said, because "I just happen to know it, and I don't have time in one life to learn another one and write at the same time. Though the one I know is probably as good as another." Home was of the heart. "That's a funny word, home. It can mean anything—an apartment, a rented room for that matter. All of it's home for me."

Yet this art, which has no place in Southern life, is almost the sum total of the Southern artist. It is his breath, blood, flesh, all . . . . We seem to try . . . to draw a savage indictment of the contemporary scene or to escape from it into a make-believe region of swords and magnolias and mockingbirds which perhaps never existed anywhere . . . the writer unconsciously writes into every line and phrase his violent despairs and rages and frustrations or his violent prophesies of still more violent hopes . . . . I do not believe there lives the Southern writer who can say without lying that writing is any fun to him. Perhaps we do not want it to be.
(Faulkner's unpublished introduction to The Sound and the Fury)

In 1947 he had not published a book in five years. He appeared that year before Ole Miss students in a series of informal lectures, the only time he ever spoke there. A. Wigfall Green of the faculty invited him. "I have never lectured," he said, "I can't lecture, and I won't lecture." But when it was agreed that no faculty members would be present and no record made of his answers to questions, he consented. As it turned out, one of the students took notes. They are presented briefly here for the flavor of the subjects.

The South was too closely tied to the other American states, he told the students, for it to have a fate of its own: the South's fate was the nation's. He

would not predict the future of the United States, but he was sure of what would transpire in his fictional Yoknapatawpha—the Snopeses would drive out the aristocracy. In response to a question about female poets, he said he liked Sara Teasdale, Emily Dickinson, Elinor Wylie, and Edna St. Vincent Millay, but he thought no one was writing good poetry anymore and that, as a symptom of the time, women had started writing detective stories. He advised young writers to set aside part of their time to be introverts. But they must not await a certain environment or mood that would be conducive to writing; they must find *time* to write. Anyone who says that he hasn't the time to write is lying to himself. Depend on inspiration to this extent: when inspiration comes, jot it down. Travel is not necessarily a preparation for writing. "Homer did okay without it." Just talk to people. The best training for writing is reading. Read everything. Preparation for writing must be in the library. In answer to another question, he said the experience of having lived in a boarding house is neither good nor bad except that the writer might want at some time to write about a boarding house. A. Wigfall Green later summarized his reply to another question on his assessment of contemporary American writers.

In his opinion, he and all the others whose names had been coupled since they had begun to write had failed: Hemingway, Wolfe, Cather, Dos Passos, and Steinbeck. Wolfe made the grandest failure because he had a vast courage—courage in that he attempted what he knew he probably couldn't do; he banged around "like an elephant in a swimming pool"; he wrote as though he didn't have long to live—and Faulkner showed humility at the mention of Wolfe's name. Hemingway had always been careful and had never attempted anything he could not do; he had been like a poker player who plays close to his vest; he had never made mistakes of diction, style, taste, or fact; he had never used a word the meaning of which couldn't be checked in the dictionary. Faulkner once had great hopes for Caldwell,

but now he didn't know. He would rank the group: Wolfe first; then Dos Passos, Hemingway, Cather, and Steinbeck. When a student called the writer's attention to his failure to rate himself, a faculty infiltrator said, "I'm afraid you're taxing Mr. Faulkner's modesty." But he rearranged his list: Wolfe, Faulkner, Dos Passos, Hemingway, and Steinbeck. (With modesty and only upon the insistence of the class Faulkner ranked—and perhaps underrated—himself.)

As such things transpire, these remarks made their way to the wire services, and Hemingway was furious. Believing his rival had impugned his physical courage, he asked a general he had known in World War II to write Faulkner about Hemingway's bravery. When the general did so, Faulkner wrote a reply, generous to Hemingway, emphasizing that his Ole Miss observations had pertained only to artistic chances and failures. Hemingway, to put it gently, remained unappeased.

On November 10, 1950, the word arrived in Oxford that he had been awarded the 1949 Nobel Prize for Literature (the prize not having been awarded the previous year). It was the fifteenth anniversary of his brother Dean's death by airplane crash. Faulkner had been to visit Dean's grave at St. Peter's Cemetery that day before receiving the dramatic phone call from New York. Mac Reed, his friend the druggist, went down to his house that day. "He was in his pasture with a beat-up jeep and mechanized equipment used for the distribution of slag. He looked awfully dirty and ragged." He never looked in Reed's direction as he circled the pasture, but after a while he turned off the motor and approached him. Reed wordlessly shook his hand. He said, "Mac, I still can't believe it." He did not want to go to Stockholm for the ceremonies, but people persuaded him that his refusal would deprive his sixteen-year-old daughter, Jill, of a trip to Sweden. Before they left Mississippi for New York en route to Stockholm he went on a colossal binge. The family

watched him nervously for days, then held a brief conference at which it was decided to push the calendar ahead and tell him it was Monday instead of Friday and that he had to sober up. He grudingly began drinking less, then happened to ask where his stepson Malcolm was. "At the high school football game," someone said. Faulkner sat up and looked around. "Somebody's been deceivin' me!" he said. "They don't play football games on Monday. I've got three more days to drink."

"He'd been on a deer hunt, drinking heavily," Maggie Brown elaborates, "and everybody was trying to sober him up." She and her husband were asleep at around 11 p.m. when Bill Fielden, Estelle's son-in-law, telephoned. "Ross, how about us bringing Pappy over to play a little pool?" Ross Brown said by all means, and should he give him a drink? "No, not even a Coca-Cola." When Faulkner got there he began rummaging around the bar looking for the light. "I think he knew all along we were sobering him up. You know, he wasn't dumb," Maggie says. They stayed up until 1 or 2 a.m. shooting pool. The next day on the plane he wrote his acceptance speech.

The *Oxford Eagle* ran the front-page headline: Nobel Award for Literature Comes to Oxonian. In a subsequent issue appeared a full page notice paid for by the Ole Miss Dry Cleaners, Gathright-Reed Drug Company, the A.H. Avent Gin and Warehouse Company, and Miller's Cafe among others: Welcome home, Bill Faulkner. "We want to tell people everywhere—Oxford, and all of us, are very proud of William Faulkner, one of us, the Nobel Prize winning author." The page displayed several photographs. There was "Count No 'Count" in Stockholm with the King of Sweden, walking in the snow, crouched before a sled chatting with "a little Swedish lad." On his return he gave his Nobel medal to his mother Maud without telling her, leaving it surreptitiously behind in a cigar box where she kept her sons' childhood mementos, such as newspaper clippings of graduations, letters from summer

camp, sketches of baseball players, wooden carvings, even a rock Dean had once brought her.

In its determined optimism his Nobel speech provided a much-needed boost to United States pride and confidence at the height of the Cold War. After that his influence became pervasive. The State Department sent him on several international tours as a goodwill ambassador. He was studied world-wide, was translated into numerous languages, and in many respects became a citizen of the world. The Republic of France awarded him its highest distinction, the Legion of Honor, the first time an American writer was so selected. It was subsequently awarded also to William Styron. As for the town itself, it cautiously began to bask in the attention, and perhaps there was, too, a subtle remorse at not having supported him when he needed it earlier.

In the years since his death in 1962 there has been in his hometown the inevitable softening, a singular amalgam of emotion involving pride, puzzlement, fear, mystery, forgiveness, and—in some quarters—a most begrudging acceptance. Is this nothing if not American, a nation whose poets are best honored when dead? A few years ago I stopped in on Sauk Center, Minnesota, where for years Sinclair Lewis was pilloried and reviled, and where now as one drives off the interstate highway into town on Sinclair Lewis Boulevard an immense sign near the Sinclair Lewis Museum proclaims not just "Main Street" but "The *Original* Main Street." Asheville, North Carolina, would not allow Thomas Wolfe to come back; his last, posthumous book was aptly called *You Can't Go Home Again*. Now there is a Thomas Wolfe Memorial Plaza across the way from the boyhood home and museum.

To this day some in the town say that Oxford did not really begin to look upon him seriously until MGM arrived in 1949 to film *Intruder in the*

I decline to accept the end of man. It is easy enough to say that man is immortal simply because he will endure: that when the last ding-dong of doom has clanged and faded from the last worthless rock hanging tideless in the last red and dying evening, that even then there will still be one more sound: that of his puny inexhaustible voice, still talking. I refuse to accept this. I believe that man will not merely endure: he will prevail. He is immortal, not because he alone among creatures has an inexhaustible voice, but because he has a soul, a spirit capable of compassion and sacrifice and endurance. The poet's, the writer's, duty is to write about these things. It is his privilege to help man endure by lifting his heart, by reminding him of the courage and honor and hope and pride and compassion and pity and sacrifice which have been the glory of his past. The poet's voice need not merely be the record of man, it can be one of the props, the pillars to help him endure and prevail.

From Faulkner's Nobel Prize address

Dust, affording the local citizens the multifold titillations of Hollywood: bit parts for homegrown actors, outside money, and the daily festival of the filming. Bill Faulkner himself had always remained somewhat aloof, ignoring the local disaffection toward him. Now *Intruder* had brought $250,000 into the county economy and suddenly everyone liked him a little better. Angered by money swaying the town's opinion of him in this regard, he at first refused to attend the world premier showing of the film at the Lyric Theatre but relented when his Aunt 'Bama, Mrs. Walter McLean of Memphis ("When Aunt 'Bama dies, either she or God's gonna have to leave heaven"), telephoned him and made him go.

Prominently inscribed today on an outside wall of the Ole Miss library are the words from his Nobel Prize address: I decline to accept the end of man . . . I believe that man will not merely endure: he will prevail. In August 1987 a ceremony was held in Oxford to celebrate the U.S. Postal Service's issuing a commemorative Faulkner stamp. There was considerable irony in this, too, and the present Oxford postmaster, James Harmon, tried to place that in perspective: "I think he had his mind on other things."

Yet one can still perceive an old, smoldering animosity, the remembrance of a long-ago slight, a buried enmity, a pent-up bitterness never reconciled. Faulkner would refuse to greet you on the square. People said he doctored his book manuscripts at the last moment, changed his words and characters in afterthought to make as much money as possible, lied and cheated for money. Had not his own daughter said in a television documentary that he once told her in his drunkenness that no one ever remembered Shakespeare's child? Who did he think he *was*? One aged town father still says William Faulkner did not like him because he thought him a Snopes. "Well," he says, across the years, "I didn't like *him* either."

In 1970, eight years after Faulkner's death, Lawrence Wells, now the proprietor of Yoknapatawpha Press, came to Oxford from Alabama as an Ole Miss graduate student. His typewriter broke down shortly after his arrival, and he looked in the Yellow Pages and found: *Varner Typewriter Repair.*

Wells found the shop just off the square and went in with his typewriter. "Mr. Varner was a one-armed, gnarled, balding, hard-faced denizen of Yoknapatawpha. I loved him at first sight. As he started working on the typewriter, I thought to myself, the Varners have fallen on hard times. They once owned Frenchman's Bend before they took over Jefferson." Wells held his peace as the man concentrated on the machine, then asked, "Did you know Mr. Faulkner has a Varner family in his books?"

"I wouldn't know," the repairman said. "I wouldn't waste my time reading his books. They're trash."

"Looking into his wasted face and hearing the flat nasal voice," Wells remembers, "I thought of the characters in *The Hamlet* and *The Town* and *The Mansion,* the harshness and bleakness of their existence, the fierceness of their spirit. I said to myself, 'My God, there really *is* a Yoknapatawpha.' "

Oxford is a serene and lovely town of about 11,000 people—roughly one-fifth of them black—and were it not for Ole Miss, with its student population almost as large as the town's, it would be a more or less typically isolated northern Mississippi county seat. Faulkner himself purposefully did not place the University in his fictional Jefferson. He put it in "Oxford," 40 miles away. He did not wish to complicate his pristine Southern town with a university.

This is the Deep South. The milieu is a world's or perhaps a civilization's remove from, let one say, Hannibal, Missouri, to which I recently paid my spiritual deferences. I stayed in "the *beautiful* Holiday Inn Twainland." The Mark Twain brand name greeted one on trucks, store windows, and marquees. There was a commercial "haunted house," a wax

museum, a Huck Finn Shopping Center, and a Twainland Express departing at regular intervals from the Mark Twain Dinette, which offered special plates of golden fried chicken named after Huck, Tom Sawyer, Aunt Polly, and Becky Thatcher, but none, if I ascertained correctly, after Nigger Jim. At the high school they were having the Becky Thatcher Relays. There had been somber talk, I was to learn, of a Mark Twain Heritage Theme Park, which would feature Huck's Sandwich Shanty, Aunt Polly's Vegetable Garden, and a Halley's Comet mine shaft and planetarium.

There is no Faulkner Boulevard in Oxford, although there *is* a murky little passageway named "Faulkner's Alley" where the bard took his shortcut to Mac Reed's drugstore, and which runs inauspiciously between Shine Morgan's Furniture Store and a health food establishment on the square. His portrait was displayed at the local McDonald's, along with Ronald McDonald's, when the restaurant first opened. Two Faulkner relatives complained, and for a short while the picture was removed. A proposal some time ago to paint the words *"Oxford: Home of Ole Miss and William Faulkner"* on the water tower was voted down, and the owner of a motel who had the notion to name several rooms after Faulkner's characters was diplomatically dissuaded. It should be pointed out in the interests of historiography, however, that when the first bar in town opened at the same motel, in 1978, it was colloquially known for a time as the "Count No 'Count," but in the absence of any sign saying so, that appellation soon faded into oblivion. Some years ago the Chamber of Commerce erected two billboards thirty-odd miles away on Interstate 55 and one on State Highway 6 declaring Oxford "the most cultured town in North Mississippi" and the home of Faulkner and the university, but these, too, did not go uncriticized . . . not a single business bears the William Faulkner brand, unless one considers the Flem Snopes Corporation, now mercifully defunct. And if an indigenous restaurateur ever does attempt to offer Quentin Compson fried chicken, Lucas Beauchamp grits, Mink Snopes catfish, or Ike McCaslin hushpuppies, he will do so at his own risk.

"The town is deliberately low-keyed on Mr. Bill," Mayor John Leslie says, "because he was an intensely private man, and we know he'd prefer it that way. Also, this is the desire of the family," meaning Jill Faulkner Summers, Faulkner's only child, who lives in Charlottesville; Dean Faulkner Wells, the only niece; and Jimmy Faulkner and Chooky Falkner (spelled without the *u*), the nephews, who live in Oxford. Richard Howorth, the owner of Square Books, which sells about a thousand Faulkner novels a year, mostly to visitors, agrees with the mayor about the town's subdued treatment of its most famous citizen. "The mystique shouldn't be exploited," he feels, "because then it wouldn't be a mystique." Chooky Falkner, son of Mr. Bill's brother John, hopes Oxford does not change. "We don't need whiskey jiggers with Brother Will's picture on them." Leslie gets numerous letters addressed merely to "The Mayor" from visitors who have come to the town because of Faulkner. "Half of them give us hell about our casual, dignified approach. The other half congratulates us." The complaints involve the lack of directional signs and historical markers pertaining to Faulkner. "They also raise cain about his grave not being marked. Hell, he wouldn't *want* it marked, would he?" Sometimes, however, the criticisms exhibit a more existential nuance. One such letter said: "You didn't like him when he was living and you still don't like him when he's dead. You're all Snopeses after all."

Picking the Bones

EVERY SUMMER OLE MISS SPONSORS A WEEK-long Faulkner conference, which usually comes right after the Ole Miss cheerleading and baton twirling clinics and draws a large group of Americans and foreigners. It is an arcane blend of graduate students, high school and college teachers, book collectors, literary scholars, biblio-philes, old ladies from Ohio, ex-existentialists, fanatics, psychiatrists, nurses, marketing analysts, pharmacists. One summer there was a homicide detective from Chicago. A dentist from Staten Island attends regularly. The 1988 conference, for instance, had delegates from 33 states and 18 foreign countries. Usually there is a substantial representation of Southerners, especially Mississippians, who may have recently been, say, to Paris, where Frenchmen upon learning of their origins had asked them only about the Mississippi River and William Faulkner; apparently they are so embarrassed by not having read much of his work that they return home and sign up for the conference. Since its beginnings in 1974, its themes have included The South and Yoknapatawpha; Faulkner, Modernism and Film; Faulkner and the Southern Renaissance; Faulkner in International Perspective; New Directions in Faulkner Studies; Faulkner and Humor; Faulkner and Women; Faulkner and Race; Faulkner and Pop Culture;

Faulkner and Religion—and there are titles to scholarly papers presented at the conference which in their allegoric and symbolic and metaphorical convolutions elude this layman's more primitive faculties.

The cultural hazards can be unusual. A Frenchman engaged in a monograph on Christian existentialist symbolism in the later works was taken on a tour of the countryside. "I am fascinated by your peasants!" he exclaimed. Years ago an Italian woman who had known Hemingway was taken to the old Carter-Tate house, a ruined unpainted shell with broken windows and vines ensnarling the porch. "Such marvelous decadence!" she said. "If you just had a *preservative* for all this decadence!" One summer I myself was having a talk at a cocktail party with an obliging Russian gentleman. I asked if there were many Snopeses in the Soviet Union. "There are none," he replied sharply. "Under the Soviet system it is impossible to have Snopeses."

Among the founders of the conference and director since its beginning is Evans Harrington, from Jones County, Mississippi, a gentle and admirable man who loves writing and literature. "They feel they're walking right into the world of Faulkner's fiction and they are," he says. "They're mystified by the gravel roads, the country hamlets, the kudzu. The Japanese, in particular, love the summer cotton. They always ask permission, then cut off the blossoms and take them home and preserve them. The Japanese also say: 'Could you take me to honeysuckle? Would you take me to it? I want to touch it and smell it.'" A man from the Midwest told Harrington that the moment he crossed over into Mississippi he was frightened. "I could just *feel* the water moccasins in your streams." At the start of one of the conferences Harrington told the assembled outlanders: "Maybe to feel Faulkner you have to be a Southerner. Some of these characters may seem quaint to you. Of Mrs. Compson in *The Sound and the Fury*, we'd say down here she *enjoyed* poor

health. You may find that strange." Afterwards a young man pulled him aside and said, "I'm from Queens. I thought he was writing about *my* mother." In the outlying hamlet of Taylor, the visitors, as if on an anthropological excursion, observed six or seven locals conversing on benches outside the general store and catfish place. "I can't understand a word they're saying," a woman from Switzerland said, "but I love that Faulknerian music."

Dean Faulkner Wells and her husband, Lawrence, live in Miss Maud's house, a block south of the square. Her father, Dean, was the youngest of the four brothers; ten years separated him and Bill. The bond between Dean and Bill was exceptionally close, marked by a fierce loyalty. It was one of the warmest and most significant relationships in Faulkner's life, and the most tragic.

"Dean was like a little wren," Ben Wasson remembered, "darting in and out of the room, constantly asking Bill about his lessons or, perhaps, about how a particular Boy Scout knot should be tied." As he grew older, Dean would brook no derogatory remarks in the town about his brother. "Whenever Bill's name was mentioned," Ethel Sweeney Duncan, a friend of that time, recalled, "Dean frequently and emphatically stated that Bill is going to write the Great American Novel." In his turn, Faulkner was immensely proud of Dean's energy, fun, self-confidence, and irreverence, his athletic prowess, his grace as a hunter and pilot. Dean was a Mississippi Tom Sawyer if ever one existed. His grade school teachers, instructed to mark an *X* on report cards next to "trait to which attention is called," gave him *X's* on: Wastes Time. Capable of Doing Much Better. Work Shows Falling Off. Inclined to Mischief. Annoys Others. Whispers Too Much. When Faulkner returned from Canada after World War I, the townspeople saw him and the youngest sibling peregrinating together about Oxford: he in his RAF suit

*T*here were railroads in the wilderness now; people who used to go overland by carriage or horseback to the River landings for the Memphis and New Orleans steamboats could take the train from almost anywhere now. And presently Pullmans too, all the way from Chicago and the Northern cities and the Northern money, the Yankee dollars arriving between sheets and even in drawing rooms to open the wilderness, nudge it further and further toward obsolescence with the whine of saws; what had been one vast unbroken virgin span was now booming with cotton and timber both....

From "The Bear Hunt"

with swagger stick, Dean in his Boy Scout uniform. Later the two of them, often with their nephew Jimmy, with whom Faulkner was also very close, played golf, usually barefooted, on the singular Ole Miss course, the one that shared its fairways with the university cows. Here young Dean was already known for his ambidextrous swing and his trick shots. On one occasion, as remembered from family stories handed down and with overtones of Faulkner's last book, *The Reivers*, Dean's daughter recounts this trip to the big city; her father was twelve, her uncle twenty-three:

There was not a great deal to do in Oxford, Mississippi, in the early fall of 1919. This would seem especially true if one had only recently returned from "the war." One night, therefore, to escape an ice cream party at the Methodist church—they were the center of all social activity in Oxford—William decided to take Dean to Memphis with him. He borrowed a car and off they went. When they arrived in Memphis, William went straight to the Red Light district on Beale Street, parked in front of one of the houses, and both of them went inside.

Years later when Dean told the story to his wife, Louise, he laughed aloud at his naïveté. At the time he had been amazed at how well William knew "the lady who owned the house and had been pleased to be introduced to her just like a grown-up." He remembered that he was allowed to stay in the front parlor and visit until "all the pretty ladies came in." Then he was sent outside to wait for William.

In Boy Scout camp at Waterford, eighteen miles north of Oxford, in the summers he would write Maud. "Mother Please get my bat out of Billies old room and send it to me. You can not get across the levey." His baseball ambitions were to spend five years in the minor leagues and five in the majors, and although this aspiration was never realized, he became a deft left-handed outfielder, fast and with a good arm, for the Ole Miss Rebels.

There was a story-book climax to the Ole Miss-LSU Tigers game in Oxford in April of 1930, which could only have amused his oldest brother who had just published *Sartoris* and *The Sound and the Fury*, with *As I Lay Dying* due out in the fall. The father, Murry Falkner, was sitting in the front row along the third-base line. The valiant Rebels were behind by two runs with two men on and two out in the bottom of the ninth inning with Dean at bat. Mr. Falkner shouted to the son, "Hit me a homer and I'll give you the car." From the account in *The Mississippian*: "Dean Falkner stepped up with his old bat loaded with a sizzling blow special for the occasion and delivered. Two men scored and Dean came around as the ball got through the center fielder." When Dean crossed home plate, there was the father waiting with the car keys in his hand. For some time after that the citizens of Oxford would see Dean driving children all over town in his "new" Buick convertible.

When all four brothers were flying planes, their mother would laugh and say, "I don't have a son on earth." When Dean was old enough, William let him use his Waco cabin cruiser and paid for his flying lessons. When Dean married Louise Hale, daughter of a successful farmer and landowner, Sanford Hale, William proposed a toast to her at the announcement dinner: "To the best wife of the best flier I have ever known." By all testimony Dean was a superb pilot with a skillful and delicate touch. He did passenger runs for Captain Vernon Omlie of Memphis, who had also taught William. He likewise became an accomplished stunt pilot, doing air shows in the Tennessee-Mississippi-Arkansas area and soliciting paying passengers at these events for short plane flights.

It was during one such event, on November 10, 1935, that the accident occurred. Dean had taken three young men from Thaxton, twenty-two miles east of Oxford, on a "one dollar" ride. The causes of the accident would remain a mystery. The Waco crashed in a wooded area and was

totally destroyed, ripped into pieces, "the four occupants so torn and mangled," brother Murry remembered, "that it was impossible to tell which piece of sheared flesh and bone belonged to whom. It was hard enough for Bill and John to tell Mother that her youngest son was dead; it would have been brutal beyond reason to allow her to see the pitiful heap that remained of him." Dean was flying the airplane, the controls on his side. Some witnesses claimed to have seen the fabric covering a wing flapping before the crash. Some said part of a wing had fallen off in the air. "The plane looked like an accordian," one of the first people to reach the site remembered. "The wings were rolled up and torn all to pieces. The plane was spinning to the left, and it hit in a left-wing spiral. Dean caught the brunt. It was not pilot error." William went to Pontotoc, a neighboring town, and helped the undertaker assemble his brother's body in a bathtub. He refused to let his mother open the coffin for viewing. As his brother lay in state in the closed coffin in the home on South Lamar, a dozen or so little boys of the town who had known him stood silently on the sidewalk in front of the house.

Bill Faulkner was traumatized. "I doubt if anything ever happened to Bill that hurt him as much as Dean's death," Murry believed, "and I think this is especially true because, in a real sense, he held himself responsible." He had paid for his brother's flying lessons and had given him full use of his airplane. "John and I tried to make Bill realize that what he had done for Dean was what he wanted above all else; his love for airplanes was so great that, given a choice, he would prefer to end his days on earth just as he did." William wrote the inscription for Dean's tombstone in the old Falkner plot in St. Peter's cemetery, the same words as on Lieutenant John Sartoris's stone in *Sartoris*: I bare him on Eagles' Wings and brought him unto me. In his horrendous grief he moved for a time into his mother's house to help look after Dean's young widow, Louise, who was five months

pregnant. During this painful time he wrote part of *Absalom, Absalom!* on the dining room table, around which some of the Faulkner family and I now gather for family feasts. Not long after the crash, as he and Ben Wasson were driving from Hollywood to Oxford, with Faulkner behind the wheel of a new Ford, he adamantly said: "We've got to get to Mississippi." During the long trip home he wordlessly drank a succession of pint bottles of bourbon. Wasson noticed tears on his cheek, and at nights in the motels heard him call out Dean's name. "There was no way for me to console him, and I had sense enough not to try." He took care of young Dean, who was less a niece than a daughter. Fifteen years later, when she asked him what her father was really like, he said: "Your father was a rainbow."

Faulkner loved the playfulness of life—sipping bourbon in the chilled twilights in the big woods, playing the host in ceremonial moments. He would say to his sister-in-law Louise, Dean's wife, "Always have $50 in the bank. You can meet any situation." When she first met him in 1934, she was not aware of his prominence as a writer. "His two favorite things were children and animals. He was also very funny." Shortly after her marriage she, Dean, and Bill went to Memphis to see the movie *Lives of the Bengal Lancers* with Gary Cooper and Franchot Tone. "It was a torture movie; they were burning people's fingernails off with acid, and Bill and Dean were laughing all the way through it." One night at Rowan Oak they were all cooking grits in a pot on the stove. The grits exploded, the lid blew off. "There was grits on the floor, the walls, the ceiling, in Nanny's hair, on all of us. He laughed until he couldn't walk." Years later he would take his niece to the Charlie Chan movies at the Lyric Theatre on Saturday nights, and as they walked home he would ask her, "Dean, did you like what Number One Son did?" and they would discuss the action in earnest detail. No one was to interrupt him when

108

he was writing, but Dean burst in one afternoon when she was in college and shouted, "Pappy, I've got the best news! An Ole Miss girl has just been named Miss America!" He pulled himself up from his writing table, took his pipe from his mouth and said, "Well, Missy, at last somebody's put Mississippi on the map."

He had a profound regard for tradition. He gave Dean's daughter Diane an American flag shortly before her second birthday. He cherished Christmas and the Fourth of July, and he had fun at Halloween with all the kids. The latter was an occasion for his storytelling, and he created an annual ritual which the Faulkner children and their friends looked forward to. With all the lights turned off at Rowan Oak, and two big jack-o'-lanterns flickering on either side of his front steps, he gathered the children around him for a ghostly tale, usually about Rowan Oak's blithe spirit, the lovely and doomed Judith Sheegog, daughter of the original owner of the house. Judith was said to have committed suicide over an unrequited love affair with a Yankee soldier and was subsequently buried under an ancient magnolia at the end of the front walk. As an accompaniment to this, there would be the faraway sound of rattling chains, and a mysterious white sheet moving about out under the giant magnolias. After terrifying his listeners with an account of Judith's demise, her unsanctified burial, and consequent hauntings, he would challenge the children to approach the ghost's dark grave with a single lit candle as protection against the spirit. "Don't anybody want to visit Judith?" His niece Dean remembers, "On this night of the supernatural Pappy would sit on the steps with you and the other costumed children clustered around him, all eyes wide in the flickering candlelight. He sat very straight, his shoulders squared, his legs crossed. His hands were still, except for occasional, deliberate movements of his pipe. His voice was low and soft, and he spoke rapidly, even though you knew the story as well as he. You

would be drawn to him by the sound of his voice as much as by the magic of his tale." She believed every word of the Judith story, and did so until she was a grown woman.

He enjoyed the spontaneity of the young and felt deeply the vulnerability of children; people should believe in their progeny. Oxford citizens recall seeing him in his Ford roadster parked at the curb in front of the grammar school many afternoons waiting for his beloved daughter Jill to get out of class for the day. His Boy Scouts had loved him, and Jill's friends respected and admired him. "Pappy could be most difficult with adults," Jill would remember, "but he had a world of patience with children"—and her childhood friends also called him "Pappy." He described himself as the "world's oldest living sixth-grader." Billy Ross Brown, son of Maggie and Ross of the Minmagary days, says that when they were together doing things, "he always treated us as equals and never talked down to us. He'd take up for us." Howard Duvall of Oxford, another contemporary of Jill's, recalls how he guided their games, played with them and showed the boys how to make rubber guns. They were not awed by him as a writer. "We were only curious mainly as to why he didn't go to work at eight o'clock and come back at five like the rest of our daddies."

His solicitude for the children extended to their teenage and university years. W. S. Shipman, Jr., was a student at Ole Miss in 1938 and recalls introducing himself to Faulkner in the haberdashery on the square; the author said he knew Shipman's father. He took Shipman and his Ole Miss companions hunting and fishing and told them stories about moonshiners and dogs and horses and, of course, of his "flying days" in France in World War I. He went to a small campus gathering of five or six of them and answered their questions about other writers. Once some Ole Miss boys wrote him that they had heard he was paid $10 per word published. "We are

sending you herewith $10. Please send us your best word." He answered: "Thanks."

When Jill and her friends were older he had hayrides, dances, and spend-the-night parties for them. When Billy Ross Brown was fourteen he and "Pappy" spent whole days at Sardis Lake working on the ballast of the houseboat, *M/S Minmagary.* "We were always carrying on some kind of foolishness, talking about things. Mr. Bill once said he was going to get some liquor distributor to sponsor me swimming across the whole lake, take out ads and make some money off it." Sometime in the late 1940s Faulkner asked Billy Ross to help him lay out some land between his and the Brown property for some fox hunting; he had acquired a relish for that ritual calling while in Virginia. The two of them, a fifty-one-year-old man and a young boy, got aerial photographs and topographical maps and pored over them together for days on end. "I think one reason he liked fox-hunting," Jill remembers, "not only for the dress-up part, was the element of risk. It appealed to him. I think it appealed to him in everything." Frequently Faulkner would telephone Billy Ross and tell him to meet at a farm supply store in town to look over material for fences; his name and telephone number is still penciled on the pantry wall at Rowan Oak from those boyhood times. They spent hours plotting the project: "Bringing fox-hunting to Mississippi," Billy Ross says. Later, after a long stay in Charlottesville, Faulkner was alone and ran into Maggie and Ross Brown in Grundy's Restaurant just off the square and asked them to have supper with him. "How's Billy Ross?" he asked. "Just fine," they replied. "Ain't but one trouble with Billy Ross," he said. Taken aback, Maggie inquired what it was. "He ain't mine."

On New Year's Eves at Rowan Oak he would invite the young people Jill's age, where before a roaring fire, as the chimes of the courthouse down the way sounded midnight, he would serve them champagne and give the toast: "Here's to the younger generation. May you profit from the mistakes of your elders."

Rowan Oak, named after the Scottish legend that a branch of the rowan tree when nailed to one's door will keep out evil spirits, was his refuge for thirty-two years. It had been built in the 1840s in a secluded grove of serene oaks and cedars at what was then the edge of town, surrounded by the rolling, wanton, path-crossed Bailey's Woods. When he bought it in 1930, during his incredibly productive time, for $6,000, it lacked running water and electricity. "Everybody in Oxford had remembered that Pappy's father ran a livery stable," Jill says. "He had lived in this house not too far up from the livery stable. So this was just a way of thumbing his nose at Oxford, you know." The house was on Old Taylor Road. The official city designation was Garfield Avenue. To him South Lamar, the main north-south boulevard, was, from the old times, *South Street,* and the parallel South Eleventh Street was called *Second South.* His friend Mac Reed remembered that in inviting people to a barbeque on his grounds, he would give these instructions: "You leave the Square and come down South Street to Old Taylor Road. Turn right. Go on Old Taylor Road uphill a piece and go west until the road starts to bend left. Look to the right and see my place back in the cedars." Then he described another route: "Come off the Square and get on Second South. Stay on it until you come to Old Taylor Road. Turn right and follow as I told you for the other way."

His workroom was downstairs: an Underwood portable on a table by a single window with a lonesome vista of the rich warm grass of the lawn and the stable and the undulating tangle of Bailey's Woods, a daybed, a bookcase, a mass of books in a second bookcase, dozens of unopened book parcels, an opened manilla envelope with a letter and application form encouraging him

Through the bloody September twilight, aftermath of sixty-two rainless days, it had gone like a fire in dry grass—the rumor, the story, whatever it was. Something about Miss Minnie Cooper and a Negro. Attacked, insulted, frightened: none of them, gathered in the barber shop on that Saturday evening where the ceiling fan stirred, without freshening it, the vitiated air, sending back upon them, in recurrent surges of stale pomade and lotion, their own stale breath and odors, knew exactly what had happened.

From Dry September

to apply as a student to The Famous Writers' school in Connecticut, a mantelpiece cluttered with ornamental bottles, ashtrays, a tobacco pouch, a comic painting of a mule, and somewhere in the room, maybe, a half-empty fifth of Jack Daniel or Old Crow or Forester. "He typed, as was his custom," Ben Wasson recollected it, "from his handwritten first draft. He would discard unsatisfactorily typed pages in a wastebasket to one side of the desk. As he pecked away with two fingers, he usually had the stem of his pipe clenched tightly between his teeth, making his mouth seem even smaller and thinner."

William Styron, visiting there, once described the interior. The library just opposite the living room or parlor

is a spacious, cluttered, comfortable room. A gold-framed portrait of Faulkner in hunting togs, looking very jaunty in his black topper, dominates one wall; next to it on a table is a wood sculpture of a gaunt Don Quixote. There are gentle, affectionate portraits of two Negro servants painted by "Miss Maud" Falkner.... Around the other walls are books, books by the dozens and scores, in random juxtaposition, in jackets and without jackets, quite a few upside down: The Golden Asse, *Vittorini's* In Sicily, The Brothers Karamazov, *Calder Willingham's* Geraldine Brandshaw, the Short Stories of Ernest Hemingway, From Here to Eternity, *Shakespeare's* Comedies, Act of Love *by Ira Wolfert,* Best of S.J. Perelman, *and many more beyond accounting.*

A few blocks to the north and east of Rowan Oak is St. Peter's Cemetery. It was to here, when he was thirty-three, that he carried in his lap the tiny casket of his firstborn child, Alabama (named after his Aunt 'Bama), who died when she was nine days old.

"The cedar-bemused cemetery," as he described the one in Jefferson, is only a few blocks from the Square: the stones "whiter than white itself in the warm October sun against the bright yellow and red and dark red hickories and sumacs and gums and oaks like splashes of fire itself among the dark green cedars." As with most small-town Southern places even today, the cemetery is integral to the daily life of the town, to its abiding spirit and memory, existing both apart from and together with its commerce and habitude. The living and the fictitious are not strangers here. There are surnames on the stones here that are the same as his fictional characters, giving to this terrain a poetic, unearthly ambience.

Walking among the stones, as I often do, it is not difficult to imagine the idiot Benjy on his weekly visits in *The Sound and the Fury*. The inscription from Proverbs under the marble face of Eula Varner Snopes, wife of Flem Snopes, atop one of the grandest stones in the Jefferson cemetery, is nearly the same as that to Faulkner's grandmother on an equally formidable monument in the old Falkner plot: "Her Children Rise and Call Her Blessed." In the black section, which borders upon the white and mingles here and there with it, lies the grave of Mammy Caroline Barr, the indomitable woman who raised the Falkner boys. He wrote the inscription on her tombstone: Her white children bless her.

His own stone is a rather simple one. He lies next to his wife, Estelle, under some oaks at the slope of a gentle hill. Bill Appleton, the supervisor of St. Peter's, has found strange objects left here by visitors: flowers, candy kisses, pints of bourbon, and once a soggy volume of the collected poems of William Butler Yeats. Many times he has seen literary pilgrims at the grave after midnight with flashlights. Once I myself found a Hallmark greeting card on the grave signed by a gentleman from Denver, with the handwritten salutation "Have a Good Day," and later in a glorious and lustrous forenoon of mid-March with the golden wildflowers abounding I spied several young Ole Miss students, boys and girls, in sober meditation.

But the town also attracts scholarly adventurers of a more serious persuasion who come and stay as long as they can and become imbued with the Faulknerian compulsions. One among many was Masaru Inoue, a forty-four-year-old scholar and college professor, who came from Yokohama to Yoknapatawpha on a year's sabbatical. He had discovered *The Sound and the Fury* twenty years before in Japan and had re-read it ten times. He saw parallels between Faulkner's characters and his own ancestors. His grandmother had tried to cling to the illusion of the old times when her ancestor was governor of a prefecture. "That was about 380 years ago," Masaru says. "My grandmother always told me that when she saw the rich people who lived in front of us in Osaka City she remembered we were different, at least in the mind and spirit. The other people were like the Snopeses. She tried to forget the poverty we had. It was a matter of pride and dignity. Carolyn Bascomb Compson and my grandmother were living in the same situation." Inoue's great-uncle was killed in a civil war in 1877. "That was only twelve years after your own Civil War. He was shot by the Japanese National Army. My side, in a sense, were the *rebels*." Masaru became so immersed in Faulkner's world that he felt it a part of his own life. He came into the town for the first time on a bus from Memphis. "We crossed South Lamar. I saw the white building with the clock above it. I moved my eyes and there was the Confederate soldier. On the other side of the courthouse was the First National Bank, which William Faulkner's grandfather established. I saw the water tower. 'Oh, this is it,' I thought. 'This is it!' I really felt I was *home*."

We took Masaru out in the Delta, my native ground, driving its flat straight euphoric roads from Sledge on the north to Yazoo City on the south. I enjoyed viewing the landmarks of my past through the eyes of the visitor who knew the Delta through Faulkner's work. It was harvest time; stray cotton bolls lined the roads, particles of the dry, clean cotton seemed to float in the very atmosphere. "When I saw the cotton fields," he wrote his family in Japan, "they looked to me like *snowfields*. And I felt, this whiteness made slavery, as Faulkner knew so well. He wrote of the children sired from the black slaves: 'They endured.' "

I was with Masaru when he saw his first Mississippi jackrabbit and his first rattlesnake and possum, and when he went on his first deer hunt. "It was dark in the woods. I looked up into the sky. It was ghost-like. There were no leaves, only branches. I made no sounds, no noises. I just waited, as Ike McCaslin did." He wished to experience the four seasons—"not Vivaldi's, but Faulkner's"—and the musical cacophony of crickets and katydids of summer reminded him of Gail Hightower. The honeysuckle in April evoked *The Sound and the Fury*. The wisteria in May was *Absalom, Absalom!* "Last year in late August we had really cooler days, as William Faulkner said. I walked to the Yoknapatawpha Press and asked Dean Faulkner Wells, 'Are we now in *Light in August*?' She kindly answered, 'Yes, Masaru, we are.' You can imagine how excited I was."

There are hazards, however, in such spiritual immersions. One early evening in June Masaru saw his first fireflies. He stood watching them, mesmerized; they took him, he said, to the world of *Absalom, Absalom!* An upstanding Oxford citizen telephoned the police to report that a suspicious Oriental had been standing in his parking lot for an hour, as if entranced by some dark vision. The constabulary swiftly arrived. "They didn't know what to think at first," Masaru says. "But they were gentlemanly when I told them I was looking at the fireflies to feel the atmosphere of this strange, wonderful town."

Sole Owner and Proprietor

THE CONVERGENCE OF FACT AND FIC-tion from the Faulkner corpus is often eerie, but titillating. The Oxford telephone directory, for instance, lists fourteen Varners, even including a Jody Varner, two Hippses, seven Ratliffs—one of them on Old Highway 6 in the mythical Frenchman's Bend vicinity—six Littlejohns, two Bundrens, thirteen Carotherses and twenty-two Houstons (Mink Snopes killed the intolerable Jack Houston). There is one Barron, one Sartor, which is a mere syllable from "Sartoris," and the Benbow Village Apartments. Irwin Shaw once claimed to me that he acquired more than a few of the names of his characters from the box scores of European rugby matches. Bill Faulkner did not have to go that far.

The real-life Lowe twins, Ed and Eph, played the Gowrie twin brothers in the movie *Intruder in the Dust*, and one can see them to this day, older yet even more uncannily identical at sixty-five, dressed precisely alike as they stride in exact step toward Smitty's Restaurant on South Lamar, or with binoculars wordlessly looking down together from a second-floor window upon the courthouse square. There is an aging black man here—he once served a stretch in Parchman for murder—who has sporadically and unsuccessfully been digging for gold (said to have been buried when Grant came through the county on his Vicksburg campaign) in and about the ruined plantation houses in the countryside, just as various Yoknapatawpha entrepreneurs did around the Old Frenchman's place. The same black man, who spends considerable time in the jail, during his most recent incarceration used his one allowable telephone message to call "Cap," the white, eleven-year-old son of friends of mine, to raise the $250 in bail money to set him free. Cap himself is the living personification to me of young "Chick" Mallison, who along with his black comrade Alexander and Miss Eunice Habersham dug up graves at night in *Intruder in the Dust* to exonerate the black farmer Lucas Beauchamp of murder.

The Mississippi Delta begins thirty miles west of Oxford; the hills descending into the flat alluvial black land as into some dark, enigmatic valley, as if dropping out of a mountainous spine into a brooding land of mists and shadows with its violent twisting rivers called Yazoo, Tallahatchie, Yalobusha, Coldwater, and the place names Issaquena, Itta Bena, Midnight, Satartia, Pentecost, Swiftown, Pugh City, Egypt, Brazil, Indianola, Darling, Tunica, Mound Bayou, Savage, Panther Burn, Hushpuckena. With notable generic exceptions, and despite a lingering antebellum myth, it was only thinly settled by the outbreak of the Civil War and retained much of its inchoate frontier flavor up to the turn of the century. It was to the eastern edge near Batesville that the young Faulkner was first invited to General Stone's deer-and-bear lodge. The Big Woods were gradually cut back and destroyed until only the triangle formed by the Yazoo and Mississippi Rivers two hundred miles south near Yazoo City remained, and this surely is the setting for old Uncle Ike McCaslin's last hunt in *Delta Autumn*, to me one of the most beautiful and stunning short stories in the language. Faulkner was obsessed by the Delta, by its cruel and infamous Parchman Prison, by its timeless fear and beauty and power, and by the violent, majestic Big River at its western edge. Some of his finest writing is set there:

This land which man has deswamped and denuded and derivered in two generations so that white men can own plantations and commute every night to Memphis and black men own plantations and ride in Jim Crow cars to Chicago to live in millionaire's mansions on Lake Shore Drive; where white men rent farms and live like niggers and niggers crop on shares and live like animals; where cotton is planted and grows man-tall in the very cracks of the sidewalks, and usury and mortgage and bankruptcy and measureless wealth, Chinese and African and Aryan and Jew, all breed and spawn together. . . .

It was not merely fortuitous that Faulkner was intrigued by the Delta—most Mississippi hill country people have always been. He needed, I believe, the exotic, unregenerate, profligate, hedonistic, tormented Delta as a counterpoint to his more severe and unextravagant hills. Delta people, he told Ben Wasson of Greenville, are "rich like the Delta soil. And maybe self-satisfied. The hill folks think all you people are godless and headed for fire and brimstone. I expect most Deltans are touched with hubris."

Along its deepest north-south axis—160 miles—as David Cohn of Greenville wrote, the Delta begins, not literally but certainly spiritually, in the lobby of that grand mistress of the South, the Peabody Hotel in Memphis, and ends on Catfish Row in Vicksburg. Faulkner himself embroidered that appropriate analogy: "Mississippi begins in the lobby of a Memphis, Tennessee hotel, and extends south to the Gulf of Mexico." And indeed he was no stranger to Memphis, which has forever been the unofficial capital and magnet of north Mississippi and a tangible extension of the Delta and its capricious and fluctuating cotton fortunes; many of his scenes are set, too, in Memphis: in *Sanctuary, The Town*, and his last one, *The Reivers.*

Nearer home, in Oxford, the recognizable landmarks from the fiction still abound. The bronze plaque set in the white facade of the courthouse itself bears the words from *Requiem for a Nun*:

But above all the courthouse; the center, the focus, the hub; sitting looming in the center of the county's circumference like a single cloud in its ring of horizon, laying its vast shadow to the uttermost rim of horizon; musing, brooding, symbolic and ponderable, tall as cloud, solid as rock, dominating all: protector of the weak, judicate and curb of the passions and lusts, repository and guardian of the aspirations and the hopes . . . .

Directly to the south of this axis is the granite Confederate soldier on his stone pedestal, the original plans having been to place him on the north side, but Faulkner's grandmother, a community leader, was infuriated, insisting that a Southern soldier had to face south, and of course she prevailed.

A block north of the courthouse was the jail, which quartered the murderers, thieves, and moonshiners from the fiction, replaced in the year of Faulkner's death by a bland, green-and-white concrete structure. Only a few blocks west toward the university is the old railroad depot, deserted and unused now, scene of so much feverish activity in the books. A quarter of a mile or so from this place of ghosts is the black section called Freedman Town, the unpaved roads and flimsy shacks of which have now yielded to asphalt streets, federal housing projects, Martin Luther King Jr. Drive, and the town's integrated junior high school. Here, at the civic park and athletic complex, are the integrated baseball and basketball games and tennis matches. Then, back toward the square again, on the unhurried, shady streets with their antebellum houses set on broad private lawns, there will be *The Sound and the Fury* house, surrounded by magnolias, bereft now of the iron fence behind which a retarded young man similar to Benjy Compson once

walked up and down. He is remembered in real life to this day by many townspeople. Beyond this house is the Neilson-Culley home, which some claim as Miss Emily Grierson's in "A Rose for Emily," and where my friend Patty Lewis, who now lives there, says she sits on the back terrace under the magnolias with a tall drink at dusk and imagines Miss Emily and Homer Barron together in the cool dark of the upstairs in the days before Miss Emily went to the store to buy the arsenic.

It is the countryside, however, even more than the town, that is the most powerful testament to the lingering fable. All around, in the proper seasons, is the mingling cachet of the raw Yoknapatawpha earth, and the baying of the hunting hounds in the far distance, as in *Sartoris*: "mournful and valiant and a little sad." At the old College Hill Presbyterian Church, where William and Estelle were married in 1929 and where Sherman encamped 30,000 troops before he and Grant moved in their circuitous route toward Vicksburg, there is a solitary stone obelisk in the graveyard with the inscription "The Dead." Farther out this road was the mythical Sutpen place and, farther yet, the hunting camp in "The Bear" and Wash Jones's cabin. Somewhere in the piney woods running parallel to the paved farm-to-market road is the sunken road long known to locals as "the Reivers Road."

Out at the other end of the county is the village of Taylor with its post office and galleried store buildings. "Nicky, Snake, Al, and the boys," says an artist friend from the Delta, Jane Rule Burdine, who bought her old farmhouse here, "hang around in front at Mary's general store and catfish place telling tales and lies at the very spot where Temple Drake stepped off the train and into trouble." The store smells resolutely of tobacco and coffee and frying catfish. "You can't find the real Snopeses in stores like them anymore," a percipient Oxford denizen observes. "Today they live in big houses with white columns." Along the narrow winding roads with gullies

*I*t's a hard country on man; it's hard. Eight miles of the sweat of his body washed up outen the Lord's earth, where the Lord Himself told him to put it. Nowhere in this sinful world can a honest, hardworking man profit. It takes them that runs the stores in the towns, doing no sweating, living off of them that sweats. It aint the hardworking man, the farmer. Sometimes I wonder why we keep at it. It's because there is a reward for us above, where they cant take their autos and such. Every man will be equal there and it will be taken from them that have and give to them that have not by the Lord.

From As I Lay Dying

and ravines and patchy hills of scraggly cotton and corn and soybeans and the tenacious and all-consuming kudzu vines are the little tin-roofed houses and unpainted cabins, their dusty yards full of rusted derelict cars and chickens and dogs and junk and clothes drying on fences and lines. Way out in Beat Two, close to Cypress Creek in its modest and murky meanderings, is a Pentecostal church of vinyl siding with a Pascoe sign on it, this having replaced the earlier church, and in back is an old cemetery with the graves, as the county lore has it, of the real husband and wife whose fictional counterparts fused the two branches of the Snopes clan. The man subsequently deposed William Faulkner's grandfather, "the Young Colonel," as president of the bank—J.W.T. Falkner precipitously and furiously withdrawing all his money in cash and carrying it in a wheelbarrow across the square in unencumbered view of the citizens to deposit it in the other bank. This man and his wife then later purchased the Murry Falkner house on North Lamar. Not far from this Pentecostal cemetery, near a wide bottom, is William Faulkner's farm, "Greenfield," 320 acres, which as irony would have it he bought in 1938 from the same man who ousted his grandfather. Faulkner installed a black caretaker in the homestead on his farm; the banker in turn indignantly removed his mother's coffin from the family cemetery behind the house. The McCaslin and McCallum places were somewhere around here, and on a matchless day of virgin spring in front of the abandoned and collapsing farmhouse there are violets on the hills, and broomsage, and near the sagging gallery, vintage jonquils coming up, planted there many years ago by the women of this lost dwelling.

"Dark House" was the working title for *Light in August,* and this haunted countryside around Oxford is dotted with crumbling houses darkly resonating the past and the vanished people who once lived in them, and I sense the author was as possessed by them as Poe was of being buried alive—the stirrings of old twilight conversations, of mute possessions and fears and loves in the gone charters of time. On the long drive out to Yocona, twelve miles southeast of Oxford as Frenchman's Bend was to Jefferson, one traverses a successive ridge of hills much like those Mink Snopes and the sheriff crossed the day the sheriff came out to Frenchman's Bend to take Mink back to Jefferson after he killed Jack Houston. The Yoknapatawpha River—"water moving slow through the flatland"—was the old name of the Yocona River. Once, at the end of a meager abandoned road through seared corn stubble, I came on the ruined iron bridge on the Yocona, which must have been the fictional one across the Yoknapatawpha in *As I Lay Dying.* Darl Bundren's description of what greeted me—"a scene of immense yet circumscribed desolation filled with the voice of the waste and mournful water"— was as vivid and unmistakable in life as it had been in the fiction I had read thirty years before. In the nearby dying community of Tula, across the river south of the Frenchman's Bend vicinage, is a collapsing building that tilts at a precarious angle. Surely this had to have been Varner's store! Just up the hill is a neat two-story house with red shutters. Could this have been Mrs. Littlejohn's hotel? I paused at the rotted window of the store, looking into the dank shadows. I did not have to close my eyes to imagine Jody Varner and Flem Snopes holding forth there on just precisely how best to make money.

Once, years ago, I was on a Delta Airlines plane from Chicago to New Orleans at 35,000 feet. From my window, in a tender haphazard reverie just south and east of Memphis, I suddenly sighted Oxford itself far below; I recognized it immediately from the contours of the Lake Sardis reservoir, and from the Ole Miss football stadium. From the high heavens there was Yoknapatawpha County all laid out for me, very tiny from here, its woods and fields and streams and hamlets, a little postage stamp indeed of native

soil, and in my God's view of it I acknowledged: it is funny and beautiful and part of the earth, and a lot of mischief took place down there.

Racism and poverty had forever been his native state's twin burdens, and in his deepest blood Faulkner knew them both. In the heart of his fiction over the years it was the Snopeses and their allies who exerted the most ruinous influence on human society; it was the blacks who, through their quiet courage and dignity, endured. As a person, he respected and cared for black people, even though he was most surely a product of the paternalistic deep Southern world of his youth. Mammy Caroline Barr was a second mother. Toward his farmhands, Billy Ross Brown remembers, "He was the kindest soul in the world, . . . warm and generous." Willie Wilson, who lived and worked on the farm, called him "a fine man, a good Samaritan—a book writer and money maker." Another of the old hands once said, "I think he was better at writin' than farmin'."

The literary scholar Walter Taylor, himself a Mississippian, poses the argument that Faulkner never truly liberated himself, or his fiction, from this Dixie paternalism, although he honestly attempted to do so: he never adequately confronted the evils of the aristocratic planters as the greatest abusers of blacks, ascribing that instead to the redneck Snopeses. In *Absalom, Absalom!* Thomas Sutpen, the ultimate degrader of slaves, is an *arriviste*, atypical of the rest of the Yoknapatawpha patrician caste, the Sartorises and de Spains and Compsons. Having grown up in the comfortable and rigidly segregated pre–World War I Mississippi society, the brooding and sensitive young Faulkner must have been at times dubious of his own great-grandfather's—the Old Colonel's—aristocratic genesis, he who had appeared in Mississippi, it seemed, from nowhere, as suddenly as a Sutpen, or indeed even as a Flem Snopes. The young writer, too, as Walter Taylor has noted,

must have pondered from time to time the irony, if that is what it was, that his grandfather, the Young Colonel, ousted from his own bank by an allegedly Snopesian personage, deigned to link himself politically with the most strident and brutalizing redneck racists of his era, the Vardamans and Bilbos and Russells.

Still, is it not the great tortured labyrinth of his work, its power and nuance and spirit and all which resides in the corpus of it, that matters? "It can be said," Robert Penn Warren wrote, "that Faulkner began with the stereotype of the Negro, but ended by creating a human being." "A cosmic reformer," in his friend James Silver's phrase, "not from intention but because he helped to clear away much of the mythological debris of southern racial prejudice." And that which is left to the persevering reader, in Malcolm Cowley's admonition, is to perceive one of his most consistent and impressive themes: "The belief in Isaac McCaslin's heart that the land itself has been cursed by slavery, and that the only way for him to escape the curse is to relinquish the land." And that the proponents of slavery and secession, in that dark curse, "built not on the rock of stern morality but on the shifting sands of opportunism and moral brigandage." The work of itself abounds in the rich truths and harkenings and complexities, the Dilseys and Beauchamps and Christmases, the severance the society inflicts on two seven-year-old boys who are comrades, one white and one black, and that to Roth Edmonds is the "day the old curse of his fathers, the old haughty ancestral pride based not on any value but an accident of geography, stemmed not from courage and honor but from wrong and shame descended to him"; and aging Ike McCaslin, in the last finger of the vanishing Mississippi Delta woods, tells Roth Edmonds's black mistress to go north and marry one of her own kind: ". . . the instant when, without moving at all, she blazed silently down at him. 'Old man,' she said, 'have you lived so long and forgotten so

much that you don't remember anything you ever knew or felt or even heard about love?' "

He was, of course, sensitive to the race issue—and its native political context in his state—but was ambivalent about it personally for a very long time. "In those days," as Walker Percy remembered, "it was a case of the Southerners having the problems and the Northerners criticizing the Southerners. And Faulkner, when he was criticized or when he was approached on the wrong angle on this, would react in an old-fashioned, Southern way."

It is easy, in A.D. 1990, to forget the cruel and ponderous racial climate in the Deep South—and especially in Mississippi, the deepest of the deep—in the 1950s and early 1960s. These were the very bad times for his state—"sweltering with the heat of injustice," as Martin Luther King, Jr., said then of it, "sweltering with the heat of oppression." In the early 1950s there was a burgeoning fear, quite frenzied in its unfolding, that the federal courts would intervene in the segregation of the public schools.

The 1954 Supreme Court decision on the integration of the schools introduced a new day fraught with violence and tension. For many whites it spelled doom; the savagery would worsen with time. At stake was the soul of the state, and meaningful dissent was all but impossible. The daily newspapers in Jackson, the capital city, were likely the most openly and virulently racist of any in America. Six months after the Supreme Court decision, the white citizens of Mississippi approved by a five-to-one margin a constitutional amendment tightening voting requirements; the amendment, in effect, made it impossible for blacks to register to vote. Soon after this, the voters approved by two-to-one another amendment authorizing the state legislature to abolish the entire public school system if this were deemed necessary to prevent integration, either locally or statewide. These were the result of the general hardening of opinion, as well as the lobbying of the White Citizens Council, composed largely of prominent professionals and businessmen, an organization which Hodding Carter, Jr., would call "the Ku Klux Klan with a clipped mustache."

There was a resurgence of lynchings, all of them unsolved. A fourteen-year-old black boy visiting the Delta from Chicago was murdered for whistling at a white woman; the white men indicted for the crime were unanimously acquitted. Subsequently a State Sovereignty Commission, subsidized by official funds, established an extensive network of paid informers and set up secret files on hundreds of private citizens. (One can only imagine the file this incipient boondocks Gestapo had on Bill Faulkner.) In the entire state only three or four lawyers would publicly admit that Mississippi would sooner or later have to accept the Supreme Court decision. With rare notable exceptions, the white people of the state were entrusting their votes and support to anxious, marginal, visionless men, inconstant and cynical and unmanly men, who came exceptionally close to destroying Mississippi. This was the backdrop against which Faulkner would begin speaking his opposition to racial injustice in his state in the 1950s.

James Silver, the historian, was a New Yorker who arrived at Ole Miss in 1936 fresh out of Vanderbilt. Silver had long felt that Faulkner "had been writing for me all along, even sometimes about my own problems and values. But most of the time Faulkner, in his flashes of brilliance, was able to illuminate for me my own obsessive inquiry into what made Southerners act as they do." His wife Dutch became good friends with Faulkner's step-daughter Cho-cho—Victoria Franklin Fielden. "In those days," Silver recalled, "Faulkner was an amorphous and to me an awesome figure, jealously protected by his family, and out of town most of the time. Little love was lost between the community and the Faulkner household." Over a

*O*nce (it was in Missis-sippi, in May, in the flood year 1927) there were two convicts. One of them was about twenty-five, tall, lean, flat-stomached, with...china-colored outraged eyes—an outrage directed not at the men who had foiled his crime, not even at the lawyers and judges who had sent him here, but at the writers, the uncorporeal names attached to the stories, the paper novels—the Diamond Dicks and Jesse Jameses and such—whom he believed had led him into his present predicament through their own ignorance and gullibility regarding the medium in which they dealt and took money for, in accepting information on which they placed the stamp of verisimilitude and authenticity...there would be times when he would halt his mule and plow in midfurrow (there is no walled penitentiary in Mississippi; it is a cotton plantation which the convicts work under the rifles and shotguns of guards and trusties) and muse with a kind of enraged impotence, fumbling among the rubbish left him by his one and only experience with courts and law....

"*Old Man*" (From The Wild Palms)

period of time the two men became comrades and, in a genuine sense, collaborators. "Each saw in the other something that appealed to him," remembers Dr. Chester McLarty, who knew them both well. "Jim saw Bill as the great writer he was. Bill, who didn't particularly like academics, saw in Jim a man who was absolutely fearless. He began to share his liberal outlook." In the late 1940s Faulkner and Silver began interminable private discussions on the race question in Mississippi. "His position was close to mine," Silver said, "that of a moderate who understood the inevitability of the future, one who rather desperately hoped to help his section prepare for what was on the way." Faulkner had also been talking with Hodding Carter, Jr., the intrepid editor of the Greenville *Delta Democrat-Times*, and the pair had agreed that Mississippi and two or three other Southern states would be the last holdouts against any modicum of change.

With the Nobel Prize he had become a public man. In his international travels as a cultural representative of the United States to Greece, Japan, the Philippines, and South America, he was what Silver called "a real patriot who learned of an increasingly enlightened world opinion which he accepted and reflected." One day at Rowan Oak Silver saw him toss into his wastebasket a telegram from W.E.B. Du Bois challenging him to a public debate, "another evidence that he considered himself neither activist nor extremist." Occasionally he exercised bad judgment, as when he made the bizarre statement that under certain circumstances he would join his fellow white Mississippians in shooting Negroes in the street, a statement he later strenuously denied. "All in all," Jim Silver reflected, "he was—perhaps justly— attacked by the radicals on both sides. His chief desire was to have his state avoid the violence that later erupted with Meredith at Ole Miss. At the same time he understood that blacks would in time become completely integrated into American society."

Faulkner believed that the South must expiate once and for all its past sins. One could interpret in him, as Robert Penn Warren observed of his books, "a desire for black forgiveness, which the white man longs for." He wrote numerous letters-to-the-editor. "The whites have already lost their heads," he said. "Let's hope the blacks don't." On the death of Emmett Till: "Any society that condones the killing of little children does not deserve to survive, and probably won't." In 1954, in his third-person autobiographical essay, "Mississippi," in *Holiday Magazine*:

But most of all he hated the intolerance and injustice: the lynching of Negroes not for the crimes they committed but because their skins were black. . .; the inequality; the poor schools they had then when they had any, the hovels they had to live in unless they wanted to live outdoors: who could worship the white man's God but not in the white man's church; pay taxes in the white man's courthouse but couldn't vote in it or for it; working by the white man's clock but having to take his pay by the white man's counting. . .; the bigotry which could send to Washington some of the senators and congressmen we sent there and which would erect in a town no bigger than Jefferson five separate denominations of churches but set aside not one square foot of ground where children could play and old people could sit and watch them.

At Silver's encouragement in 1955, Faulkner spoke at the famous meeting of the Southern Historical Association, along with Dr. Benjamin E. Mays of Morehouse College, at The Peabody in Memphis, the first integrated event in The Peabody's history. "To live anywhere in the world of A.D. 1955," he declared, "and be against equality because of race or color is like living in Alaska and being against snow." He continued:

We accept contumely and the risk of violence because we will not sit quietly by and see our

native land, the South, not just Mississippi but all the South, wreck and ruin itself twice in less than a hundred years, over the Negro question.

We speak now against the day when the Southern people who will resist to the last these inevitable changes in social relations, will, when they have been forced to accept what they at one time might have accepted with dignity and goodwill, say, "Why didn't someone tell us this before? Tell us this in time?"

Several concerned Mississippians met with Faulkner at Rowan Oak as the state's political climate worsened, including one P.D. East, publisher of *The Petal Paper*, in a suburb across the river from Hattiesburg, which within a year of his editorship had a local subscription list of exactly zero. I later knew P.D. East in Texas; he was a flamboyant yet somber figure, tall and gaunt and anguished, who looked somewhat like Abraham Lincoln must have after a bad night's sleep. He had arduously campaigned in his paper against the Klan and the Citizens Council, irritating official Mississippi by such proposals as to change the state symbol from the magnolia to the crawfish and by running Senator James O. Eastland's name only in lower case, so that it came out: james o. eastland. With Faulkner's backing, East, Silver, and others published one issue of a journal satirizing white supremacy, *Southern Reposure*. East came to Oxford several times for this purpose, and as he and Silver crewed Faulkner around Lake Sardis one day in his sailboat, Faulkner after a long silence turned to East and asked, "Well, Mr. East, anybody put any dead cats on your front porch lately?"

Will Campbell, then the director of religious life at Ole Miss, recalls going to Rowan Oak with East and others to plan the *Southern Reposure* issue. In Mississippi back then anyone posing a threat was an "outside agitator." Campbell remembers Faulkner standing in a room looking out the windows and cracking his knuckles and saying, "Yes, I'd like to write for this. I'd like to write about Moses the outside agitator wandering around forty years in the Tallahatchie bottoms waiting for the old people to die off and then lead the rest of them to the Promised Land." When the maiden, and final, issue of *Southern Reposure* was published, hundreds of copies were addressed to leading people in the state and East trucked them to Jackson for clandestine posting. He mistook a laundry collection receptacle for a mail box and dropped in the papers, then realizing his blunder had to wait hours for the laundry truck driver. "It was the most inept counter-revolution that ever happened," observed a friend of the men involved.

In these times Faulkner was more of an outcast on his home soil than Count No 'Count had ever been, and he was pitilessly attacked anew by his fellow Mississippians. "He became subject to anonymous phone calls at all hours," his brother John said. "Mysterious voices cursed him, and his mail was filled with abusive, anonymous letters." Nor did his own family like what he was saying. "Since none of us agreed with Bill's views," brother John remembered, "we said, 'It serves him right. He ought to have known this would happen.'" His brother Murry said that he "could not understand how he, whose life had been so much like my own, could have arrived at the conclusion he had expressed about integrating the schools." The "old affectionate companionship that had existed all our lives," Murry admitted, "had noticeably diminished" when his brother began expressing his views "on mixing the white and Negro races."

Brother Will Campbell, later to become a writer, who was dismissed as director of religious life at Ole Miss in 1956 for his stand on the racial issue, remembers that even five or six years after the Nobel Prize, Faulkner was still *persona non grata* on the Ole Miss campus because of his public position on race: "They were afraid of him." Faulkner had endowed a music scholarship, which was to be presented to the recipient at a concert in Fulton Chapel.

One of the vice-chancellors feared Faulkner might actually appear at the presentation. "What are we going to do if Mr. Faulkner shows up?" he fretted to Campbell. "What if he wants to make the presentation himself?"

His niece Dean remembers being with him in Jackson in 1958 and walking with him around the outside of the Governor's mansion on Capitol Street. Several years earlier, in his *Requiem for a Nun*, he had set a scene in the Mansion (Temple Drake and Gavin Stevens are trying to get the governor to commute Nancy Mannigoe's death sentence) and it was apparent to her on this day that he would have enjoyed nothing better than to be invited inside. For a Governor of Mississippi to have done so in 1958 would have courted political suicide.

In Faulkner's dwindling days he was relatively quiet, having had his say, "but he emphatically did not," Jim Silver asserted, "as his segregationist brother claimed, return to the family doctrine of white supremacy. To anyone who had read Faulkner's great novels, such a position would seem preposterous." On one of the nights he came to the Silvers' on Faculty Row of Ole Miss to watch "Car 54, Where Are You?" he was introduced to students who had come down from Harvard and Brandeis and Notre Dame to observe the South first hand, and he talked with "the utmost candor and sense. He castigated the Citizens Council, and as he had said earlier, accepted contumely and the risk of violence." Ross Barnett and his lieutenants, modern-day Snopeses one and all, as if having stepped full-born and vainglorious and grasping from the great writer's own fictional words years before, who would have seen Mississippi go down in nihilism and blood as surely as Hitler wanted it finally of Germany, had taken over the state. As the

crisis deepened Faulkner must have felt a growing degree of powerlessness and alienation. Perhaps that is why he was spending so much time away from home, in Charlottesville. Silver saw him on a visit there. "You know, Jim," he said proudly, "I'm on the faculty here."

He died less than three months before the Meredith Crisis, the Last Battle of the Civil War, as we call that terrible juncture here; the violence likely would have broken his heart. But would it have interested him to know that his young friend Billy Ross Brown would be the captain of one of the two National Guard units nationalized by Kennedy and sent in to rescue the beleaguered federal marshals on the Ole Miss campus, and his nephew Chooky the captain of the other? Four afternoons to the day before his death, he accompanied his friend Aubrey Seay, a restaurateur of Oxford, on a fishing outing to Enid Lake. They were on the water and Faulkner was looking through a pair of binoculars. After a while his companion mentioned that Meredith would soon be coming to Ole Miss. "Do you suppose we'll have any trouble?" Faulkner lowered the binoculars and replied, "If we do, it will be because of the people out in Beat Two who never went to a university or never intended to send their children to the University."

He would be gratified, I believe, by the remarkable racial strides in recent years in Mississippi, and by the civilized public dialogue on race. And surely he would be amused that his great-nephew, whom we call "The Jaybird," was one of only two or three whites on the Oxford High School basketball team in 1984, and importuned his mother to bake him cornbread so he could jump as high as his black teammates; but the black teammates came to his house to eat the cornbread, too.

The Legacy

PERHAPS IT HAS FINALLY COME FULL CIRCLE. Unless I am mistaken, the young people of his beloved Mississippi are reading him. David Sansing, the distinguished professor and in many ways the spiritual and intellectual heir at Ole Miss of Jim Silver, assigns at least one of Faulkner's books to students in his Mississippi history courses. They invariably say they want to read more. "They're awed," he tells me, "that he takes a locale, places, white and black people they know and raises them to the level of great literature. It really does something for them. It enhances their own self-esteem. He shows them that a Mississippi sharecropper or a poor black can face the same choices and mysteries as great leaders of state. He makes them aware for the first time that his people have to wrestle with the same complexities, the same inconsistencies that they do in their own lives. For the first time they realize, whether they'll be a lawyer in a small town, a doctor, a schoolteacher, a coach, that they too are in a life-and-death struggle. They tell me they're better equipped to deal with these things after reading him."

A young black woman, a Mississippian, in one of Sansing's classes had such an emotional reaction to *Absalom, Absalom!* that she was unable to write her report. Her grandfather, she told him, was white and still lived in her town. They never talked to one another. When she read about Thomas Sutpen, she said, he reminded her of her grandfather and of how evil man can be. "If Mississippians had read Faulkner thirty-five or forty years ago," Sansing says, "we wouldn't have had the problems we had."

Every historian of the South quotes William Faulkner sooner or later. His friend Jim Silver believed Faulkner was the greatest historian he ever read: "For the good hunter there is no finality. The game, in Faulkner's words, is 'not only to pursue but to overtake and then have the compassion not to destroy, to catch, to touch, and then to let go because then tomorrow you can pursue again.' I wish I had written those words about hunting, about history, or about life." "What's it like there?" the Canadian Shreve McCannon asks Jason Compson of Mississippi at Harvard in *The Sound and the Fury*. "What do they do there? Why do they live there? Do they live at all?" In 1958, six years before Vietnam, C. Vann Woodward, likewise in the Faulkner legacy, wrote that the one way in which the South is "immune from the disintegrating effect of nationalism and the pressure for conformity," the one way it has not changed, is history, for history has happened to Southerners. Quentin Compson: "his very body an empty hall echoing with sonorous defeated names; he was not a being, an entity, he was a commonwealth. He was a barracks filled with stubborn, back-looking ghosts . . ." Eudora Welty speaks of the Mississippian and his sense of place, "the sense of continuity that has always characterized us . . . the sense of generations and continuity." Faulkner as writer both drew upon and sustained that continuity. "It is necessary," Anaximander wrote 2,500 years ago, "that things should pass away into that from which they are born. For things must pay one another the penalty and compensation for this injustice according to the ordinance of time." So it was with slavery, and so too with secession and the doomed

Confederacy, and Faulkner knew this well. Shelby Foote remembers taking him to Shiloh, in which Mississippi figured so prominently, and was impressed, of a place he had studied so hard and knew so well, how much his companion knew its geographical and military factors— and its meaning to history.

Notwithstanding the universal context, much of Faulkner which interests me encompasses his native state—Mississippi—in the year 1990, as it would interest him: where it has come from, where it is going. Bill Minor, a leading columnist in the state's most widely-read newspaper, would note that it had become fashionable for Mississippi politicians to quote from Faulkner in their public speeches, especially his Nobel Prize address: "For the reformers in state government, Faulkner's affirmation of beleaguered optimism seems appropriate." The actor John Maxwell, who has taken his one-man Faulkner show "Oh, Mr. Faulkner, Do You Write?" around the United States and the world, has carried it all over Mississippi, too, not just the big cities but the small towns—Waynesboro, Belzoni, Indianola, Meadville, New Albany, Yazoo City—and echoes David Sansing about the younger generation. "Some of the older people may still to this day hold a grudge," he says, "but the younger ones, forty and under, are fascinated by him, held in his spell and what he tells them. They so much admire his courage." Recently the Mississippi Department of Economic and Community Development has been taking out large ads in the *Wall Street Journal*, *Forbes*, and other business publications with a reproduction of the March, 1989, *National Geographic* cover devoted to Faulkner's Mississippi: "a twist of irony that William Faulkner would have appreciated," a writer for the National Geographic Society observed; "the irony lies in the fact that the individuals whom Faulkner best portrayed were those ridden with guilt, corruption, and greed . . . not exactly the type of Mississippian the state

*I*t was a big, squarish frame house that had once been white, decorated with cupolas and spires and scrolled balconies in the heavily lightsome style of the seventies, set on what had once been our most select street. But garages and cotton gins had encroached and obliterated even the august names of that neighborhood; only Miss Emily's house was left, lifting its stubborn and coquettish decay above the cotton wagons and the gasoline pumps—an eyesore among eyesores. And now Miss Emily had gone to join the representatives of those august names where they lay in the cedar-bemused cemetery among the ranked and anonymous graves of Union and Confederate soldiers who fell at the battle of Jefferson.

From ''A Rose For Emily''

wishes to set forth in its bid for more industry." The state agency conducted research before this advertising campaign to ascertain what sort of "image" outsiders had of Mississippi. "People either had a negative image or no image at all," an official reported. Some Yankee respondents actually professed to physical fear when riding down the Mississippi roads, not unlike the Faulkner conference delegate whose thoughts turned to water moccasins.

David Sansing, too, speaks of "the other Mississippi" which reflects in the most inherent way the Faulkner heritage, the Mississippi not of illiteracy but of literary tradition, not of ignominy but of nobility, not of the Vardamans and Bilbos but of the John Sharp Williamses and Mike Espys, not of the Barnetts and Rankins but of the Medgar Everses and Fannie Lou Hamers, not of the prejudice and injustice and ignorance but of the humanity and charity and fidelity. "Mississippi has been a closed society for much of its history," he writes, "but it has also been one of the most closely observed societies in the western world. If Mississippi sneezes, the national media gives it a quick glance. If it sneezes twice, Europe will look. It may be that there is just no other place in America quite like Mississippi." Sansing, himself one of its brave and eloquent voices also has written:

To recognize the other Mississippi is only to say that in its darkest hours, all were not racists, all were not bigots, all did not condone what was going on, and that a few whites and many blacks called out against injustice and prejudice. And some of them, like Medgar Evers and Vernon Dahmer, and Clyde Kennard and Fannie Lou Hamer, gave their last full measure in the cause of justice and freedom and human dignity.

To recall its earlier existence is preface to the claim that the other Mississippi is now the real Mississippi, that the other Mississippians have at last taken their state back from the bigots and the racists and the reactionaries and the counter-revolutionaries and all those who think Mississippi's finest hour has passed. Some will dispute that claim, but I don't

care what anybody says, Mississippi is not like it used to be. It is different from what it was twenty-five years ago. It is better. It is not a closed society anymore. I do not claim that it is innocent of any wrongdoing. There is still prejudice and ignorance and poverty in Mississippi, and there are still acts of injustice and even violence. But those despicable acts are no longer sanctioned by the state's power structure and discrimination is no longer an official state policy.

To say all of this is not to say that the other Mississippi has won and that the battle is over. We all know that the battle will never be over. And the goal is not so much to win it, but never to end it.

Faulkner wrote about this other Mississippi before there was one. He knew it and anticipated it. He had a sense of what it might be. There are some things we ought to be against, he said: not to get our names in the paper or to make money, but because they are wrong. There is an element in the human spirit that wants to do good and be right and elevate people and promote civilization, and on his native ground he was its advocate and its representative. "Pappy cared for Mississippi and its people," his niece Dean says. "He felt the same ambivalence we do now. He hoped all his life that his state and his people would finally be better than we were. He felt a responsibility like a duty-bound first son to the people here. No matter where he was, he never got away from that. He never let us down."

"Few other American authors have been so seriously read and so appreciated here and around the world," writes William Boozer, editor of the quarterly *Faulkner Newsletter.* "No others have been so studied, perplexed over, analyzed. There is a largess of criticism today of Faulkner criticism, notably among scholars and academicians. Strollers in the middle of the road, hardcore yet lay Faulknerians, holding no briefs, mostly smile and read on, absorbing all

of it they can, separating the chaff to their own private satisfaction." From the campuses there is an unceasing harvest of theses and dissertations, with no end in sight; one can only be astonished at the prices being paid for Faulkner books, and far-flung Faulkner collections, catalogues, memorabilia have become nothing if not a sizeable industry. Recently a single letter from Faulkner in 1926 to Anita Loos congratulating her on *Gentlemen Prefer Blondes* was sold at auction for $1,900, and that is only one example. His handmade gift books to Helen Baird in the 1920s in New Orleans, *Mayday* and *Helen: A Courtship*, were valued at $100,000 a copy when an advertising executive gave them to Tulane. A copy of one of the one hundred signed, numbered editions of *Go Down, Moses* of 1942 goes for $4,000, and more. Will laundry lists and old fish hooks be next? Various collections are housed at Virginia, Tulane, Texas, Michigan, Ole Miss, and the New York Public Library, among others, and Southeast Missouri State recently acquired books and manuscripts valued at $3.5 million. Of publishing books about Faulkner there is also no end, and this, I unabashedly confess, is another one of them.

What on earth, I have pondered, would Mr. Bill, merely the gentleman farmer that he was, make of all this? Would he be amused, vexed, titillated? I suspect his reaction would likely be a chuckle, the chuckle that sounded like a snort.

It was death, to him, that was the end of it. As with most writers, from his earliest years he was obsessed with the knowledge of death. His work is suffused with death: its premonitions, fears, visions, presentiments. Late in his life he told students at the University of Virginia that a writer "knows he has a short space of life, that the day will come when he must scratch through the wall of oblivion, and he wants to leave a scratch on that wall—Kilroy was here—that somebody a hundred, a thousand years later, will see." One rainy Sunday afternoon in the 1920s he and Bill Harmon, a friend who owned a haberdashery on the square, were driving down the highway with drinks. Faulkner was telling stories and singing a morbid song—"Something to do," as Harmon remembered, "with people who put on airs as if they were the only ones in the world who mattered." He pointed to an expanse of countryside: "There," he said, "is a beautiful spot. I'd like to be buried in a spot like that—right there. You know, after all, they put you in a pine box and in a few days the worms have you. Someone might cry for a day or two and after that they've forgotten all about you." When the photographer Cofield got a request from Bennett Cerf of Random House for a color transparency of a portrait for publication, Faulkner told him, "Send him a plain black-and-white copy; otherwise someone may think I am already dead." Once, a few years before his death, he told his brother Murry that each of us will become a sort of radio wave in the hereafter. Mac Reed, his friend the druggist, was helping him mail the manuscript of what was to be his last book, *The Reivers*. As they finished packaging and labeling it, he leaned over the counter and said, "I been aimin' to quit this foolishness."

In June of 1962 he was thrown by his horse, Stonewall, on Old Taylor Road. It was a serious and acutely painful injury to his vertebrae, ribs, and collarbone. He took to bed and began drinking heavily. One afternoon the following week he painfully walked to Dr. Felix Linder's house; he and Linder had known each other since grammar school. They sat together on Linder's porch. "Felix," he said, "I don't want to die."

He died in Byhalia of coronary thrombosis on July 6, 1962—on the Old Colonel's birthday.

William Styron, a great admirer in his youth and maturity of Faulkner's work, who himself had already written *Lie Down in Darkness*, *Set This House on Fire* and *The Long March*, and was just then writing *The Confessions of Nat Turner*, came down from New York with Bennett Cerf, both Styron's and Faulkner's

*W*e have a few old mouth-to-mouth tales; we exhume from old trunks and boxes and drawers letters without salutation or signature, in which men and women who once lived and breathed are now merely initials or nicknames out of some now incomprehensible affection which sound to us like Sanskrit or Chocktaw; we see dimly people, the people in whose living blood and seed we ourselves lay dormant and waiting, in this shadowy attenuation of time possessing now heroic proportions, performing their acts of simple passion and simple violence, impervious to time and inexplicable—Yes, Judith, Bon, Henry, Sutpen: all of them. They are there, yet something is missing; they are like a chemical formula exhumed along with the letters from that forgotten chest, carefully, the paper old and faded and falling to pieces, the writing faded, almost indecipherable, yet meaningful, familiar in shape and sense, the name and presence of volatile and sentient forces; you bring them together in the proportions called for, but nothing happens; you re-read, tedious and intent, poring, making sure that you have forgotten nothing, made no miscalculation; you bring them together again and again nothing happens: just the words, the symbols, the shapes themselves, shadowy inscrutable and serene, against that turgid background of a horrible and bloody mischancing of human affairs.

From Absalom, Absalom!

publisher, for the funeral. He would subsequently write of it in *Life Magazine*. On that day he remembered the July Mississippi heat: "It is a monumental heat, heat so desolating to the body and spirit as to have the quality of a half-remembered bad dream, until one realizes that it has, indeed, been encountered before, in all those novels and stories of Faulkner through which this unholy weather—and other weather more benign—moves with almost touchable reality." The courthouse square lay drowning in "a hot, sweaty languor bordering on desperation." Nina Goolsby, the editor of the *Oxford Eagle*, had distributed around town handbills, and they could be seen on the storefronts:

IN MEMORY
of
WILLIAM FAULKNER

This Business Will Be
CLOSED

From 2:00 to 2:15 PM
Today, July 7, 1962

As the funeral procession wound around the square toward St. Peter's, the sidewalks were thronged with people, whites and blacks, in front of Grundy's Cafe, Earl Fudge's Grocery, and the Rebel Food Center. Styron was moved by this display and commented on it to a native. "It's not that they don't respect Bill," he replied. "I think most of them do, really. Even though none of them ever read a word of him. But funerals are a big thing around here. Let a Baptist deacon die and you'll *really* get a turnout." Styron reported:

Our car comes abreast of the courthouse, turns slowly to the right around the square. Here the statue of the Confederate soldier . . . stands brave and upright on his skinny calcimine-white pedestal, looking like a play soldier and seeming vaguely forlorn. Both courthouse and statue loom over so much of Faulkner's work, and now, for the first time this day, I am stricken by the realization that Faulkner is really gone. And I am deep in memory, as if summoned there by a trumpet blast. Dilsey and Benjy and Luster and all the Compsons, Hightower and Byron Bunch and Flem Snopes and the gentle Lena Grove—all of these people and a score of others come swarming back comically and villainously and tragically in my mind with a kind of mnemonic sense of utter reality, along with the tumultuous landscape and the fierce and tender weather, and the whole maddened, miraculous vision of life wrested, as all art is wrested, out of nothingness. Suddenly, as the watchful and brooding faces of the townspeople sweep across my gaze, I am filled with a bitter grief.

As the author was buried in a hot, dry field of St. Peter's, Styron remembered a poem Faulkner had written in his youth, called "My Epitaph":

*If there be grief, let it be the rain
And this but silver grief for grieving's sake,
And these green woods be dreaming here to wake
Within my heart, if I should rouse again.*

*But I shall sleep, for where is any death
While in these blue hills slumbrous overhead
I'm rooted like a tree? Though I be dead,
This soil that holds me fast will find me breath.*

In the sweep of his work his sense of the tragedy and dishonor of even the worst of human beings gradually softened, to be replaced by compassion

and pity. "Man aint really evil," the sewing machine agent V.K. Ratliff says, "he jest aint got any sense." Running through Faulkner's work is a profound recognition of the awful brevity of life, that people are only temporary tenants of the earth and at its mercy in the end. "It was the land itself which owned them," Mink Snopes acknowledges, "and not just from a planting to its harvest but in perpetuity . . . ." We are all in it together, I believe he is saying to me, and we are all in for a difficult time: "Memory believes before knowing remembers. Believes longer than recollects, longer than knowing even wonders."

We have a few old mouth-to-mouth tales; we exhume from old trunks and boxes and drawers, letters without salutation or signature, in which men and women who once lived and breathed are now merely initials or nicknames out of some incomprehensible affection which sound to us like Sanskrit or Choctaw; we see dimly people, the people in whose living blood and seed we ourselves lay dormant and waiting, in this shadowy attenuation of time possessing their acts of simple passion and simple violence, impervious to time and inexplicable.

Twenty-one years after his death, in 1983, citizens of Oxford gathered on the square to dedicate the bronze plaque bearing his words from *Requiem for a Nun* describing the courthouse. The master of ceremonies was his doctor and loyal old friend, Chester McLarty. "We gather today," he said, "to honor Bill in the personal way that is appropriate among friends. We may do so secure in the knowledge that Bill would indeed like to be recognized by the people who are so much in his debt. And, finally, with this plaque we honor ourselves. We take this means of recording for posterity our recognition of our good fortune to have had such a man among us." He always looked on his own work with great detachment, McLarty said, "and seemed baffled when others insisted on focusing their attention on him rather than on his writing." And he quoted from Faulkner's letter of 1953 to his friend Joan Williams:

And now I realise for the first time what an amazing gift I had: uneducated in every formal sense, without even very literate, let alone literary, companions, yet to have made the things I made. I don't know where it came from. I don't know what God or gods or whatever it was, selected me to be the vessel. Believe me, this is not humility, false modesty: it is simply amazement. I wonder if you have ever had that thought about the work and the country man whom you know as Bill Faulkner—what little connection there seems to be between them . . . .

As for Bill Faulkner and myself, Mississippians, I have notes before me now on him and his work and what it has meant to me, notes to myself to conclude this book with. I toss them away, for they suddenly seem self-serving: gratuitous and redundant. Out of all of them, which I wished to write, I will only say two: I have grown to love him, and he never sold out.

Acknowledgments

I must first thank Bill Eggleston, my distinguished collaborator on this book, whose vision and extraordinary sensibilities echo in every compelling image. His depiction of the rural Southern countryside speaks eloquently of the fictional world of Faulkner and, not coincidentally, the shared experience of almost every Southerner. Oftentimes lurid, always lyrical, his stark realism resonates with the language and tone of Faulkner's greatest work, invoking the mythical cosmos of Yoknapatawpha county.

His images do not require captions; indeed, captions would detract from their magic. They are images not intended to illustrate the real Mississippi but rather to evoke the Mississippi of Faulkner's fictional world. They invite participation on their own terms. In another collaborative work, *Let us Now Praise Famous Men* (1941), the writer James Agee made an important statement about the use of photographs in book form. The photographs, he said, were presented without a single word of explanation. They were, Agee wrote, "...not illustrative. They, and the text, are coequal, mutually independent and fully collaborative." The work of Bill Eggleston would have pleased Bill Faulkner and James Agee immensely.

I must also gratefully acknowledge the cooperation and assistance of various members of the Faulkner family—Jill Faulkner Summers, Jimmy Faulkner, Dean Faulkner Wells, Chooky Falkner, Louise Hale Meadow—and of many Oxford residents too numerous to mention, but especially Dr. Chester McLarty, Maggie Brown, Billy Ross Brown, Mayor John O. Leslie, William Lewis, Jr., Jane Rule Burdine, Patty Lewis, Nina Goolsby, David Sansing, Howard Duvall, Richard Howorth, Pearline Jones, Cap Henry, and Ed Morgan.

I am indebted to seven eminent Faulkner scholars—Joseph Blotner, Cleanth Brooks, Carvel Collins, Malcolm Cowley, James Meriweather, Michael Millgate, and David Minter—for their invaluable insights into Faulkner's life and work. I also warmly acknowledge John Faulkner for his reminiscences in *My Brother, Bill* and Murry Falkner for his vivid memoir of the brothers' upbringing, *The Falkners of Mississippi,* and Dean Faulkner Wells for her unpublished master's thesis at Ole Miss about the Falkner brothers and particularly about the father she never knew—Dean—and for *The Ghosts of Rowan Oak,* about her uncle and the children who listened to his ghost stories.

Evans Harrington, former chairman of the Ole Miss English Department and director of the annual Faulkner Conference, was as always generous and indispensable in his help, including our many drives through the back roads of Lafayette (Yoknapatawpha) County. I am indebted to Yoknapatawpha Press and Lawrence Wells and to William Boozer, editor of the quarterly *Faulkner Newsletter.*

Robert Frese and his colleagues at Atticus Press were guiding spirits of this book from the start. Nancy Fitzpatrick, Vicki Ingham, and Jerry Higdon of Oxmoor House were invaluable in their patient contribution in seeing this project through every step, making this book a work of art.

Many fellow writers have also been crucial to this work: William Styron, Robert Penn Warren, Eudora Welty, Walker Percy, Shelby Foote, Lewis P. Simpson, Tennessee Williams, Elizabeth Spencer, Ellen Douglas, Richard Ford, Lawrence Wells, James Seay, Will Campbell, Barry Hannah, Ellen Gilchrist, James Whitehead, Bill Minor, John Griffin Jones, Katherine Clark, among others.

Other essential sources I must acknowledge include James Silver's *Mississippi: The Closed Society* and *Running Scared;* Ben Wasson's *Count No 'Count; William Faulkner of Oxford,* edited by A. Wigfall Green and James W. Webb; "A Life on Paper," the documentary produced by Mississippi Educational Television; and Malcolm Cowley's seminal *Viking Portable Faulkner.*

W.M.
1990

Books by William Faulkner

The Marble Faun. Boston, The Four Seas Company. 1924

Soldier's Pay. New York, Boni and Liveright. 1926

Mosquitoes. New York, Boni and Liveright. 1927

Sartoris. New York, Harcourt, Brace and Company. First of the Yokanapatawpha novels. 1929

The Sound and the Fury. New York, Jonathan Cape and Harrison Smith. 1929

As I Lay Dying. New York, Jonathan Cape and Harrison Smith. 1930

Sanctuary. New York, Jonathan Cape and Harrison Smith. 1931

These 13. New York, Jonathan Cape and Harrison Smith. 1931

Idyll in the Desert. New York, Random House. Limited edition. 1931

Miss Zilphia Gant. Dallas, The Book Club of Texas. Limited edition. 1932

Light in August. New York, Harrison Smith and Robert Haas. 1932

A Green Bough. New York, Harrison Smith and Robert Haas. Book of poems. 1933

Doctor Martino and Other Stories. New York, Harrison Smith and Robert Haas. Fourteen stories. 1934

Pylon. New York, Harrison Smith and Robert Haas. 1935

Absalom, Absalom! New York, Random House. 1936

The Unvanquished. New York, Random House. 1938

The Wild Palms. New York, Random House. 1939

The Hamlet. New York, Random House. First volume in the Snopes trilogy. 1940

Go Down, Moses. New York, Random House. 1942

Intruder in the Dust. New York, Random House. 1948

Knight's Gambit. New York, Random House. A cycle of five short stories and one novella. 1949

Collected Stories of William Faulkner. New York, Random House. 1950

Requiem for a Nun. New York, Random House. A three-act play. 1951

A Fable. New York, Random House. 1954

Big Woods. New York, Random House. Four hunting stories. 1955

The Town. New York, Random House. Second volume in the Snopes trilogy. 1957

The Mansion. New York, Random House. Concluding the Snopes trilogy. 1959

The Reivers. New York, Random House. Faulkner's last novel. 1962

Essays, Speeches and Public Letters. Edited by James B. Meriwether. New York, Random House. 1965

The Faulkner-Cowley File. By Malcolm Cowley. New York, The Viking Press. 1966

Portions of the text appeared originally in the March 1989 issue of *National Geographic.*

Excerpts from: *As I Lay Dying; Sanctuary; The Faulkner Reader; The Unvanquished; Light In August; Absalom, Absalom!; Big Woods; Essays; Speeches and Public Letters;* and *Go Down, Moses* by William Faulkner. Reprinted by permission of Random House, Inc. Excerpt from *Soldier's Pay* by William Faulkner. Reprinted by permission of W. W. Norton and Co. Excerpts from *A Life On Paper* and *Count No 'Count* by Ben Wasson, *Conversations with Elizabeth Spencer* and *Conversations with Walker Percy.* Reprinted by permission of University Press of Mississippi. Excerpts from *The Falkners of Mississippi* by Murry Falkner and *On Prejudices, Predilections, and Firm Beliefs of William Faulkner* by Cleanth Brooks. Reprinted by permission of Louisiana State University Press. William Faulkner's letter to Will Lewis, Sr. Reprinted by permission of Jill Faulkner Summers. Excerpts from *My Brother Bill* by John Faulkner and "The Faulkner Newsletter." Reprinted by permission of Yoknapatawpha Press.

Library of Congress Catalog Card Number 90-61946
ISBN: 0-8487-1052-5
Manufactured in the United States of America

First Edition • LFS

Published by Oxmoor House, Inc.
Book Division of Southern Progress Corporation
P.O. Box 832463, Birmingham, Alabama 35201

Created by Atticus Press and Yoknapatawpha Press

Designed by Robin McDonald

Typeset in Schneidler by Compos-it, Inc., Montgomery, Alabama

Color Separations by Capitol Engraving Company, Nashville, Tennessee

Printed and Bound by Nicholstone Companies Inc.

Text Sheets Are 90# Finnart Matte from Äänsekoski, Finland by The Madden Corporation, New York, New York